CW01653729

Should I do a somersault in church?

A Celtic challenge to evangelicals and charismatics

RAY SIMPSON

kevin mayhew

I thank the many friends and acquaintances who have shared with me their questions, anger and insights, which I reflect in the text. These include Andreas, Brad, Davy, Howard, Jack, Pauline, Pete, Richard, Ross, Sam, Sarah, Simon, Siri, Susie, Tom, Torey and guests who chill out at our Open Gate Retreat House on the Holy Island of Lindisfarne.

Published in 2006 by

KEVIN MAYHEW LTD
Buxhall, Stowmarket, Suffolk, IP14 3BW
E-mail: info@kevinmayhewltd.com
www.kevinmayhew.com

© 2006 Ray Simpson

The right of Ray Simpson to be identified as the author of this work has been asserted by him in accordance with the Copyright, Designs and Patents Act 1988. All rights reserved.

No part of this publication may be reproduced, stored in a retrieval system, or transmitted, in any form or by any means, electronic, mechanical, photocopying, recording or otherwise, without the prior written permission of the publisher.

9 8 7 6 5 4 3 2 1 0

ISBN 1 84417 593 6
Catalogue No. 1500906

Cover design by Sara-Jane Came
Edited by Andrew Moore
Typeset by Fiona Connell-Finch
Printed and Bound in Great Britain

Contents

Who is this book for?

This book can help three groups of people: bewildered evangelicals and charismatics; liberal Christians who are dismissive of these; and Christians in Celtic renewal who want to understand how to connect their insights with both of these groups.

The seed out of which this book grew was planted when Spring Harvest, which runs Britain's biggest evangelical jamborees, approached the author. Spring Harvest are finding that many young (and not so young) evangelicals are at a crossroads and are confused as to which direction they should take. Some may have Christian parents whose culture is so remote from theirs they cannot share it; yet their natural friends may have non-Christian beliefs and morals. Do they become defensive and keep one, or both of these groups at arm's length? Or is there a way they could navigate the twenty-first-century seas, avoiding the reefs, but communicating with fellow voyagers, because God is in everyone's boat, even when unrecognised? Spring Harvest thought that perhaps Celtic Christian spirituality could enable this.

Some people are in charismatic churches, and it is dawning upon them that there are parts of life – mundane, intellectual, social, even devotional parts – that their charismatic experiences do not touch or sustain. Can renascent Celtic spirituality, which is at home with God-in-all-of-life, but does not exclude charismatic gifts, reach the parts that these do not?

This book may also help liberal Christians who don't understand evangelicals or charismatics. Perhaps they perceive them as being in a box. This book can help them get inside the box, and learn to value the love of Jesus and Scripture, the passion and missionary motivation which beats in the hearts of those inside it. Some conservative evangelicals believe that their commitment to the truth of Christ as revealed in the Bible requires them to exclude ways of being Christian that cannot clearly be defined. For them, practices that grow out of the imagination, feelings, creative arts or natural human friendship are dangerous because they can lead people astray; they are to be avoided. Liberals think that approach is intolerant, narrow and de-humanising. Both conservative evangelicals and liberals sometimes dismiss charismatics as superficial, loud people. This book may help them to avoid throwing out the baby with the bath water.

Buttoned-up Christians, whether evangelical or liberal, may be freed up by this book without losing their integrity. The author himself has not, so far, done a somersault in church, but he has learned how the stifled creativity of Christians can be born again.

The early Christian Church in Celtic lands was biblical and orthodox in its faith, yet it had a place for charismatic gifts, creative arts, and head-through-the-heart thinking. It was earthed and mainstream and, perhaps because of this, was secure enough to befriend people of all backgrounds and beliefs and to enjoy natural delights. Many people today see in a renaissance of 'Celtic spirituality' a way to remain true to fundamentals and yet to be winningly at ease with people from many backgrounds.

Each chapter unpacks a question that some evangelicals or charismatics or seekers are asking. It then looks for clues that biblical Celtic Christianity can offer, and ends with a Celtic challenge which consists of a real life story or piece of writing.

Who am I?

Question

I really want to learn how to live deeply from my true self – living out of both the good and the dark, the divine breath and the 'shit' of who I am and seeing the dark transformed – have you any exercises that I can do to help earth myself into who I really am, and to live more authentically?

I really want to know Christ deeply and to explore the meaning of faith, although I seem to have a lot more questions and doubts than certainties. I feel the Holy Spirit is pushing me out into the 'desert' and I want to work the Beatitudes into my life. But I still find the thought of going back to church a negative and constrictive feeling and probably need a while to recover. There are aspects of church life I don't want to experience again, such as formulas, prejudice, bigotry, black and white ways of explaining life, and the use of subtle guilt to make people do things.

Response

I am the child of my two parents. I am a parent or a sister or a brother and so on. I am like a hazelnut in God's hand; I only exist because God has always infinitely loved me.

We know only a little of ourselves at first. We can learn

to become at home with those aspects of ourselves that are earthy: with our bodies, our sexual, emotional, mental and imaginative responses. We can find out the sort of personality type we are. We can observe, through our interactions with others, what gives us a sense of well-being, anger or boredom and what these reactions tell us about ourselves.

We can never know all of ourselves. A man told his wife after twenty-five years of happy marriage: 'I love you more than ever but you are also more of a mystery to me now than ever.' God made us to be so wonderful that, in this life, there will always be more depths to plumb.

Our eternal destiny is to know ourselves as God knows us.

Celtic Challenge

> In this life I know to some degree.
> In the next life I shall understand fully even as I have been understood fully by God.
>
> *1 Corinthians 13:12*

> The sacred duty of being an individual is to gradually learn how to live so as to awaken the eternal within you.
>
> Eternal Echoes: Exploring our Hunger to Belong, *John O'Donohue (Bantam Books, 2000)*

Can I follow God and be myself?

Question

The people in my church told me I could not drink, smoke, take cocaine. I wanted to follow God but also to be myself. So I decided I would not give up drinking, smoking or taking cocaine unless God himself showed me I should. Even when I made a joke in church I was treated with suspicion. I want to celebrate God with the whole of my life, but they want to shut me up. What should I do?

Response

Get to know Christian groups where you can be yourself. Go to Christian network events such as (in UK) Greenbelt, Soul in the City or Spring Harvest. Flap your wings. Make new Christian friends. Find out about great, faith-inspired human beings.

Celtic Challenge

The stories told about Brigid, who brought Christianity to the sixth-century Irish, portray her as a spontaneous woman overflowing with humanity. She milked cows, galvanised kitchens, and laid spare places at the meal table for anyone who was passing by. She made ale. She told a mad person to start shouting about Christ, and he did! When the local ruler threatened to execute a man who unknowingly killed his pet fox, Brigid took a fox to the ruler in exchange for the prisoner. She raced in a carriage and, to this day, the curragh at Kildare is kept as open land where horses can be raced.

> I came that you may have life in all its fullness.
>
> *John 10:10*

Am I a worm or a princess?

Question

I was taught to believe that I am a worm. These Bible verses were quoted at me: 'I am a worm and no man' (Psalm 22:6) and 'even our best actions are like filthy rags' (Isaiah 64:6). The Church of England Book of Common Prayer has these phrases in it: 'we are miserable sinners' and 'there is no health in us.' Then I was introduced to the writings of Matthew Fox during a counselling course. He teaches that creation is good, human beings are made in God's likeness, and we should celebrate human life and creation. It made me tingle. I felt alive. Was I mistaken?

Response

I think you are a princess, though even princesses can get worms. Over a lifetime we go through a gamut of experiences. After some bad failing we may say, 'I am a worm,' and after some joyful celebration we may say, 'I am a royal child.' However, it is not wise to make a general dogma out of a particular experience.

The psalmist you quote contrasts the way humans treated him – as if he was a worm – with the way God treats him – God is always there for him. The prophet Isaiah speaks to a people who have turned their backs on God and who are therefore like leaves that are blown away. An alternative choice is available. Those who make this choice are like trees with roots which are not blown away (Psalm 1).

Celtic Challenge

Ita founded a cell church near Limerick in sixth-century Ireland. So many young people came to her discipleship school that she became known as 'the foster mother of the saints of Ireland'. She understood evil, within and without her, only too well, and undertook ceaseless spiritual warfare against it. Yet she was so fruitful, not only because of this, but also because she had a good, God-given self image which affirmed her and enabled her to affirm others.

Once she dreamed that an angel gave her three precious stones. The angel explained that these represented the Father, the Son and the Holy Spirit and that she was the dwelling place of the Holy Trinity: 'Always in your sleep and vigils the angels of God and holy visions will come to you, for you are a temple of God, in body and soul.'

These affirming experiences began when she was a child. Once neighbours rushed to help put out a fire that they thought had engulfed Ita's house. But they found the young Ita in her room which was untouched by any fire. When she arose from that room next day they said she had a beauty they had never seen before or since. The fire was the grace of God burning in her.

> You Christians are royal priests, a holy nation,
> God's own people . . .
> who have received God's mercy.
>
> *1 Peter 2:9-10*

In what way might I need roots?

Question

After doing Alpha courses I became a cell leader and I am active in our worship group. I work for a successful finance company and commute home to a lovely wife and baby. A visiting speaker at our church said I needed to develop roots. I felt angry at first, but this keeps nagging at me. Everything in my life seems fine, so in what way might I need roots?

Response

This needs some unpacking. I will suggest the WHAT, WHY and HOW of two types of root.

1. We need roots in the Christ who worked in the first Christians – including the first to become Christians outside the Roman Empire and the first to become Christians among our forebears. The New Testament records how Christianity took root within the Roman Empire. In sixth- and seventh-century Ireland and Britain we discover how Christ took root in peoples outside the Roman Empire, from whom come the roots of many of us.

   It is important to embrace this because Christians fall into the copycat trap of confusing culture with Christ. When they copy what they read in the New

Testament without understanding what belongs to the local culture, they alienate the people in their own culture whom they seek to win, and lose their own authenticity. If they can sense how Christ's presence can be expressed in a different culture they are more likely to discern how to be effective for Christ in their own.

You can grow this kind of root by reading and meditating on stories of Celtic saints, having learned about the background in which they lived.

2. We need roots in the Eternal Christ who works in the holistic, primal plane, with which the modern West, for all the good things it has achieved, has lost contact.

   It is important to embrace this because God intends us to be holistic, and the fragmentation of western society is God's judgement on us for splitting off the external achievements from the collective unconscious which we share with all people.

   You can grow this kind of root by trying to integrate what is God-given in primal rhythms. Cultivate the ceaseless prayer of the heart, prophetic picturing and intuitive wisdom. Cultivate 'ascesis', that is, the constant dethroning of our desire to control. Our ego is so strong that only a radical alternative spiritual path can reconnect us with God in the primal rhythms. By keeping daily times of quiet and seasons of prayer we can make a start.

Celtic Challenge

Celtic Christians had their eyes washed in continual contemplation. As we immerse ourselves in their stories we ourselves, insensibly at first, become rooted and grounded in that Christ-love which allows something deeper than our controlling ego to dictate our lives.

How do you become wise?

Question

How do you become wise?

Response

I knew nothing about wisdom. I put my foot in it whenever I opened my mouth. I was like a bull in a china shop. But I read in James 1:5 that if anyone lacks wisdom, and they pray for it, God will give it to them. So I prayed and, though I am not naturally wise, I have become wiser than I would otherwise have been.

In life, wisdom lies in accepting that we are not God. The enemy of wisdom is thinking we have arrived when in fact the journey has scarcely begun. The beginning of wisdom is reverence for the other, God first, then people. Wisdom sees life as a mystery to be entered into, not a problem to be solved. It lies in listening to fragile feelings, hidden voices and deep harmonies. Wisdom can distinguish between short-term urgency and long-term value.

Celtic Challenge

An evangelical bookshop owner realised that one third of the life and Scriptures of Jews, including Jesus, were dedicated to wisdom, but that Christians had neglected this. He dedicated his life to learning wisdom. One day a druid entered the shop and the owner told the druid about his new commitment. 'I have been searching for a soul friend who is dedicated to wisdom, said the druid. 'Will you be my soul friend?'

An early British ruler asked Illtyd to establish a community college to which the brightest believers in the land flocked. They learned religion, philosophy and agriculture. Illtyd was regarded as the wisest man of his time. Yet one of his pupils learned even greater wisdom. Samson used to debate the meaning of Scriptures with his mentor. When they could get no light on a matter, Samson fasted and prayed until understanding was given.

Can you be wild and born-again?

Question

I've been taught to be against New Age ideas because they are woolly and dangerous. Then a fellow student enrolled in a distance learning course of the Order of Bards, Ovates and Druids. She showed me this extract from their material:

> The wildness in ourselves is that part of us that longs to live close to nature. It is also that part of us that is inherent, not learned or acquired – the heritage of intuitive and instinctive wisdom that is our birthright. This part of us has been denied so long by a culture terrified of instinct and feeling. The denial of this Wild Self creates alienation and apathy, stress, depression, and violence. But when accepted into our lives, it transforms itself into a source of creativity and healing. Druidry encourages the Wild Self out of hiding . . . Slowly the centuries of repression begin to lift.
>
> *The Order of Bards, Ovates and Druids, PO Box 1333, Lewes, East Sussex, BN7 1HB. www.druidry-org*

This makes me feel that my Christian faith has missed out on something. Can I be wild and born-again?

Response

The question should be the other way round: Can you be born-again without being wild? Jesus informed Nicodemus that a person needs to be born again and that experience is like being blown by the wind (John 3:7-8).

The Bible warns us against worshipping what is created rather than the Creator (Romans 1:25). Our intuition and our wild self are part of what is created.

We should see these as God's presence within us. We should not trust these more than we trust what we know of God outside us, in Christ and the Bible. But we should invite Christ to free us from fear and repression, so that we may be in touch with our bodies, our creativity and nature.

Celtic Challenge

An entry in the *Anglo-Saxon Chronicle* for 891 reads: 'Three Irishmen came to King Alfred in a boat without any oars from Ireland, whence they had stolen away because they wished to go on pilgrimage for love of God, they cared not where . . . They took with them only enough food for seven days.'

I presume they took no oars because they wanted to put themselves absolutely into the hands of God, trusting that wherever the wind blew them would be the place God wanted them to be. Most people think out beforehand where they intend to go on a pilgrimage or prayer walk, but for those pilgrims the process was more important than the destination. It was an act of love.

These wanderers were in the tradition of great Bible personalities such as Abraham, who left home and family to go out into the unknown. They knew that they needed to exercise faith in order to increase it, and their voyage was a way of losing control of their situation and trusting in God alone.

People may ask 'what's the use of doing this sort of thing?' These Irish pilgrims teach us that there does not have to be 'a use' from our point of view, but that God seems to use such acts of trust in deeper ways than a human could engineer. In the case of these three Irish pilgrims, they brought the king news of the death of Suibne, the great anchorite teacher of Clonmacnoise, and it is said they went on to be of service to the king in his great project of teaching his people.

How do I get out of my box without going to pieces?

Question

I was brought up in a particular, strict church. I was taught that all keen Christians should do things our way. Then I started to go to the big Christian festivals and met Christians who do things in different ways. I've learned so much from them. I've branched out. I've even been to a Benedictine monastery. I don't want to live the rest of my life in that little box. How can I put these different insights into my normal life?

Response

Seek out what is God-given in the different strands of Christianity you meet. Then start to weave those strands together.

Celtic Challenge

Cedd was one of the first Anglo-Saxon boys to be educated at the school founded at Lindisfarne by the seventh-century Irish Mission to Northumbria. He became a fine Christian evangelist and teacher. When the ruler of the

East Saxons wanted a similar mission there, Cedd and one other were sent. He sailed down the east coast in his little currach. In 654 he arrived at Bradwell, a place very different from Lindisfarne, for here were the remains of a Roman fort and the incomers retained some of the Roman ways. Cedd never forgot or betrayed what he had learned from the Irish Mission in Northumbria, but he let Jesus show him how to relate to the East Saxons in ways that brought God alive to them. He built a church from the stone of the Roman fort even though the Irish always built churches of wood – this church at Bradwell-on-Sea is still a pilgrim centre today.

He met the local king, and in due course warned him not to enter the house of a relative who had married unlawfully, so that the king would model good values to his subjects. The king disregarded this. When Cedd next met him he stayed on his horse (this was a Roman custom), but lowered his pastoral staff to the ground (a Celtic custom) and prophesied that the king would die in that very house. The king fell to his knees and asked forgiveness, but the prophecy came true.

Perhaps because Cedd was able to exercise the authority of Christ in two cultures, as well as speak two languages, he was made the translator at the 664 Synod of Whitby, when Christians from the Irish and Roman Missions presented their opposing cases. The historian Bede drew a parallel with the Day of Pentecost, when the Holy Spirit enabled people of different languages and cultures to understand God's words through Peter. Cedd became a go-between. The Go-between has been used as a name for the Holy Spirit.

Who can I trust?

Question

I believe that Jesus is my authority and that the Bible is his word; but the Bible does not deal with modern life. Different preachers and Christian groups of opposite views claim they speak in the name of Jesus. My parents' generation hold different views to mine. How do I know which Christians I can trust, for their motives and wisdom?

Response

Jesus said, 'By their fruits shall you know them' (Luke 6:44). God may be located in Scripture, and also in common sense, conscience, the wisdom of nature and experience. In early centuries heresy (a distortion of a Christian teaching) was regarded as the same thing as the sin of self-promotion. The willingness to be humble, and to weigh with respect what is believed by Christians everywhere, is a characteristic of the person we might trust.

Celtic Challenge

This issue faced Britain's indigenous Christian leaders at the turn of the seventh century. The Celtic (indigenous) Christians were in disarray, with their backs to the wall.

Pagan forces vied with Christianity. The Christian 'clans' were divided. And now the Bishop of the capital city of the Roman Empire, who, it was said, inherited the authority of the apostle Peter, the first Christian leader in Rome, had sent a big mission to convert the Saxon invaders (later known as English). His mandate was to knock together the heads of all the Christian Churches in Britain and to create a standardised organisational approach.

Augustine, a reluctant Italian monk and the leader of the Italian Mission, landed in Kent. He asked the British bishops to meet him, but they were not sure who to trust.

So they consulted a wise and holy hermit. 'Should we accept his proposals and work with Augustine?' they asked the hermit. 'If he is a man of God, yes, you should' said the hermit, 'but if he is not, you should not.' 'How will we know if he is a man of God?' they asked. 'If he is humble and treats you with respect you will know that he is holy,' the hermit replied. 'And how will we judge if he has humility?' 'If he rises to greet you,' the hermit advised. Sadly, history records that Augustine did not honour the calling of the indigenous bishops by rising to greet them, and they did not trust Augustine's package.

How should I relate to people I disagree with?

Question

How should I relate to people who believe in things I think are wrong?

Response

Repeat these words: 'God loved the world so much that he gave his only Son' (John 3:16). Now keep repeating just the words 'God loved the world'. Now invite the Holy Spirit to make you a reflector of this divine attitude. Invite the Holy Spirit to help you FEEL this in your heart.

Question

But do I look upon such a person as an object of pity to be served or do I enjoy her company?

Response

Regard her as you would like to be regarded. Enjoy her human qualities – her fun, creativities, personality, her mind, body, soul. But be real.

Celtic Challenge

For all we Irish, inhabitants of the world's edge, are disciples of Saints Peter and Paul and of all the disciples who wrote the sacred canon (of the New Testament) by the Holy Spirit. We accept nothing outside the evangelical and apostolic teaching. None of us was a heretic . . . no one a schismatic; but the Catholic Faith, as it was first transmitted by you, successors of the holy apostles, is maintained unbroken . . . For among us it is not who you are but how you make your case that counts. Love for the peace of the Gospel forces me to tell all in order to shame both of you who ought to have been one choir. Another reason is my great concern for your harmony and peace. 'For if one member suffers all the members suffer with it' . . .

Therefore, my dearest friends, come to an agreement quickly . . . I can't understand how a Christian can quarrel with a Christian about the Faith. Whatever an Orthodox Christian who rightly glorifies the Lord will say, the other will answer Amen, because he also loves and believes alike. 'Let you all therefore say and think the one thing' so that both sides 'may be one' – all Christians.

Jesus has gathered us, is gathering us, and will gather us out of all regions, till he should make resurrection of our hearts from the earth, and teach us that we are all of one substance, and members of one another.

From Columbanus' letter on the 'Condemnation of the Three Chapters' to Pope Boniface IV in 613, written at a time when there were two power-hungry rivals for the 'Chair of Peter'.

When a friend lets you down how can you forgive and forget?

Question

Someone I trusted really let me down and I feel terribly hurt; I know we are supposed to forgive and forget but I'm not sure I can do either.

Response

Who said we are supposed to forget? Memories can be healed but they cannot be erased.

I, too, have had this experience. The first thing we need to do is to be honest about our feelings. My feelings included anger, self-pity, a desire to justify myself and induce people to condemn my friend, and a need for my friend to understand the hurt and harm he had caused. So sometimes I addressed my thoughts to the absent friend. Some of these feelings were appropriate and others were not. So I wrote what I felt in a secret journal day after day. I did not write an objective account, the aim was to get the feelings out of me and on to a page. Sometimes I also shouted them out to Jesus.

It is not possible to forgive what we have suppressed. It does not always come quickly. I used to address my absent friend, through Jesus: 'I forgive you with my mouth and my will, but my feelings have not yet caught up with my mouth and my will.'

I found out that forgiveness should not be cheap. I want God to teach my friend a lesson, not because I am vindictive, but because other people need to know the cost of their wrong actions. It took two years before I could go to sleep without the hurt searing into me. After that time, I began to see blind spots and failings in myself.

I realised that my poor communication and self-pity also needed forgiveness.

Celtic Challenge

The spiritual training exercises designed by Cummian in fifth-century Ireland advise a person who is incensed in their mind by a hurt done to them to restore the relationship by sharing their feelings with the person who has hurt them. Restoration of the relationship through contact was vital. They also suggest that a person who long harbours bitterness in their heart shall be healed by a joyful countenance and a glad heart. Praising God when feeling let down is a hard but healing practice.

> Forgiveness from the heart towards everyone.
>
> *From an eighth- or ninth-century Rule of Saint Columba.*

Should I shun everyone who's into the occult?

Question

Are all occult beliefs evil? I've been told not to have anything to do with people who get involved in the unseen world, but nowadays everyone's doing it, and some of them are nice people.

Response

The word occult refers to that which is hidden. Lots of hidden things can be good, but Christians are called to be transparent and to bring things into the light. When people refuse to bring what is hidden into the light, then we have good reason to beware.

The supernatural, as well as the natural world, is created by and belongs to God, and both need to be brought into harmony with God, that is, redeemed. That is the work of Christ whose partners we are.

Orthodox, biblical Christianity talks of five groups of supernatural (bodiless) beings or forces. First, those that are and always have been wholly instruments of God's will; these are known as angels or good spirits. Second, those who, from the moment of creation, have pulled against

God. These are known as demons or evil spirits. Third, gods made by human hands, to which supernatural powers are imputed, but which have no objective existence (e.g. Psalm 115:1-8). Fourth, personifications of human psychic forces – e.g. Mother and Father figures. These are called universal archetypes and may serve a useful purpose. Since God has made us to have dreams, in which such archetypes appear, we may conclude that God wishes us to process this psychic material prayerfully. The goddess movement can be seen as a desire to evoke the eternal Feminine which has been suppressed. A prayerful processing of this may lead us to value both the feminine and the masculine attributes in us and to give them great respect, but not worship. Fifth, there seem to be gods, or spirit beings, who can be persuaded, as can humans, to change for the better. Psalm 82 has God presiding over an assembly of the gods, and urging them to stop supporting the wicked.

To recycle an old saying, 'Why should the devil have all the best of what is hidden?'

Celtic Challenge

In a stroke of inspired genius, Patrick chose to celebrate his first Easter on the Hill of Slane. This was in full view of the place where the pagan High King of Tara, with all his druids, lit a large fire to proclaim the rebirth of the sun after winter's death. Every other fire had to be extinguished until it was re-lit from this fire. So when Patrick lit a fire in the name of the risen Christ, the future of Ireland was at stake. 'If the fire of this new religion is not quenched today, it will burn forever, and it will overcome all the fires of our religion,' the druids told the High King. Many are the legends of how God used nature's wonders to extinguish the pagan fire and to protect Patrick's life.

When the king's officers came with their chariots to arrest Patrick, he, according to one medieval *Life*, quoted Scriptures such as 'Some trust in chariots and some in horses but we will trust in the name of our mighty God' (Psalm 20:7) and 'Let God arise and scatter his enemies' (Psalm 68:1). A storm ensued, so violent that the horses and their riders fled. Although the king's men lay in wait to catch Patrick and his men as they left, all they saw passing them was a herd of deer. That is how the tradition grew that as these Christians prayed 'Patrick's Breastplate' God shielded them from their enemies' eyes and it is why this prayer is known as 'The Deer's Cry'.

What about Muslims?

Question

People in my church say I should not make close friends with Muslims, because it might draw me into false ways, but something inside me says I should. I'm confused. What do you think?

Response

No action that is based on fear is of God. The first thing is to be clear about how God wants us to relate to all people in the world. God dared to trust everyone in the world, even though some would reject him (John 3:16). We are designed to reflect God's attitude of love that reaches out to all. To do this, we have to be secure in ourselves, as God is secure in himself.

Jesus taught that God-honourers such as Abraham, though they obviously had not known him as Jesus, would sup with him in the kingdom of heaven. The apostle Paul taught that the eternal, divine Christ was involved in shaping the Jews (1 Corinthians . . .) .

So, it is vital to befriend, respect and listen to the experience of God-honouring Muslims, mindful that the eternal Christ is also involved with them.

Celtic Challenge

Some strands in Celtic Christianity have taught that what is deepest in every human being is the likeness of God. Sin has entered into human beings and has spoilt that likeness, but has not destroyed it. So we should cultivate a fellow feeling with all other people, and look for that which is of God within them.

This approach comes out in the Celtic Prayer:

> Christ in the face of friend and stranger
> Christ in the one who knocks at the door.

As a young man Mohammed felt drawn to visit a Christian monastery. There, a monk prophetically prayed over him that he would become a prophet. Columba of Iona prophetically prayed over people. Once he prophesied that a leader of a war band, a pagan who was naturally good, would come their way that day at the end of his life. The pagan listened to Columba, was baptised, and died at peace.

Many Muslims warm to Christians who are holy men and women of prayer, and are happy to receive a prayer from them.

Vishnu or Christ?

Question

I run a multi-ethnic outreach for young people. Questions come up such as these: 'Should we follow Vishnu or Christ?' 'Or both?' 'Does it matter which?' 'If someone claims their Scripture says there is only one way, why should we believe their Scripture?' How should I handle such questions?

Response

There are two approaches you can take. The first approach is to draw out what emotional or mental need a person hopes will be satisfied by giving devotion to Vishnu (or Buddha etc.). Some archetypal figures buttress our predisposition to something – e.g. violence, lust, power. Our highest, deepest and truest longing is for unconditional love. We can encourage a friend to search for an archetypal figure who most expresses archetypal love. We can explain why the cosmic Christ is supremely that figure.

The second approach is to explain that the reason the Bible says that Jesus is the way to God, is not because God is a control freak but because God wants nothing but the best for everyone.

Celtic Challenge

An orchestra can only play a symphony if each player watches the conductor.

Early Irish Christians pictured God as rather like a conductor who leads an orchestra. The spiritual beings who are included in the orchestra are those who heed the conductor. 'St Patrick's Breastplate' pictures the Trinity as the Divine Conductor. Included in the orchestra are:

Cherubim
Angels
Leaders of angels
Patriarchs
Prophets
Apostles
Holy Virgins.

What in paganism does not conflict with Christian beliefs?

Question

What in paganism does not conflict with Christian beliefs?

Response

Being a country lover.
Treating the other person as you wish them to treat you.
Kindness to creatures.
Awareness of the natural and spirit worlds.
Enjoyment of colourful ritual.
A feeling of kinship with all.

Question

What do you think are the key differences?

Response

Christians believe we need to choose between what is morally good and morally bad in the behaviour of humans and gods.

Christians recognise that in practice we are not always motivated to do good, and that we need some all-good power outside ourselves to redeem and transform us.

Question

What about the modern pagan concept of active participation in the cosmic dance of goddess and god, female and male?

Response

Orthodox Christian theologians have taught that in the heart of the Divine there is a cosmic dance (perichoresis) in which we are called to participate, from which spring possibilities, creativities and polarities, including male and female.

Christianity believes in the Divine or Eternal Feminine and in Wisdom (Sophia).

This Wisdom calls to us (see, for example, Proverbs 8).

Throughout the world, especially in Africa, and in Black-led churches in Britain, you can find Christian churches that share in the Divine Dance: dancing, dressing up and festivity.

The balance between man and woman certainly needs to be redressed.

Celtic Challenge

In recent centuries, Christians have had a poor record of relating in a Christ-like way to pagans. It was not always so. In the sixth century Christian leaders like Columba and Kentigern befriended pagans and embraced their wisdom. Columba explained that he still had a druid advisor: Christ.

A Christian writer stated that (the cosmic) Christ had been the teacher of the Britons before they had learned about the historical Christ. Many pagans embraced Christianity, since they could see that it fulfilled their best aspirations. Pagans who were control freaks opposed the new religion, however. When they did this, Christians called on God who did signs and wonders that were greater than those of pagans. A local pagan ruler named Morken tried to starve out Kentigern's community. So the community held an all-night prayer meeting. Gales followed, and Morken's grain storehouse was swept down river and was grounded beside Kentigern's faith community!

Tradition says that the famous pagan druid named Merlin, who features in the fables about King Arthur, went out of his mind after losing a battle, and wandered distraught through Ettrick forest. Kentigern, with great compassion, sought him out and cared for him. Merlin befriended Christ and was baptised.

Is there only one way to God?

Question

Can I ask you about a big issue? The headline message of some churches is 'Jesus is Lord' or 'Jesus is the only way'. The message non-Christians 'hear' is 'We are superior to you and you must join up or cop it.' They think this approach breeds intolerance and that Christians are part of the problem, not the answer to world conflict. They assume that we are belittling other great souls such as Buddha or Mohammed. So we are perceived as a religion of bigotry which does more harm than good. I don't agree with them, but I must admit I feel uncomfortable. Am I missing something?

Response

Yes. Within God, eternally, there are movements of mercy. God creates. Humans become separated from God and one another through their ego lives. So God also carries people back to a restored unity. The supreme expression inside human life of this second eternal movement of God is Jesus. But it was not Jesus as one more noble soul, one more prophet, it was God in Jesus. The second Person in the Triune God was doing this before Jesus was born on earth and continues to do it now. He wants to do it for everyone: God loves the great and noble souls who are open to the highest and best that they know, and is carrying them back to unity. It is in THAT sense, and not in any other sense, that Jesus is the only way to God. It is like saying God is the only way to God. That is not belittling or offensive, is it?

Celtic Challenge

Soon after Patrick began his mission to the Irish he won the support of Loiguire, King of Connaught, High King of Ireland. The king's virgin daughters came to bathe at a well early one morning and saw, to their amazement, Patrick and a team of priests clothed in white vestments. 'Are you real or from the other world?' they asked. Patrick encouraged them to enquire about the real God rather than about themselves. 'Since you are daughters of an earthly king', Patrick concluded, 'I wish to wed you to the king of heaven.' His reply to their question 'Who is God?' has become famous as 'Patrick's Creed'.

> Our God is the God of all humans.
> The God of heaven and earth.
> The God of the sea and the rivers.
> The God of the sun and moon.
> The God of all the heavenly bodies.
> The God of the lofty mountains.
> The God of the lowly valleys.
>
> God is above the heavens,
> in the heavens and beneath the heavens.
> Heaven and earth and sea,
> and everything that is in them,
> – in all these God lives.

God inspires all things,
gives life to all things,
stands above all things,
and beneath all things.
God gives the light of the sun,
and strengthens the light of the night and the stars.
God makes wells in arid lands, dry islands in the sea,
and places the stars in the service of the greater lights.

God has a Son and they are co-eternal
and similar in their essence
and the Holy Spirit breathes in them.
The Father and the Son and Holy Spirit are inseparable.

The Father be with us for the rest of the day.
The Saviour beside us as we work.
The Spirit within, refreshing us.

The princesses asked for instruction, cast off their sins, and were baptised. So powerful was the effect that their two druid guides were converted, one at first, the other later. The women were buried beside the well, which is now known as Ogulla well, near Tulsk, County Roscommon.

Can I be a Christian and not believe the Bible?

Response

It depends upon what you mean. The Bible is three things – I call these the 'Three R's'

1. Varied revelations from God
2. Varied responses from persons and peoples
3. Varied records of these.

It is intrinsic to Christian belief that God in many ways, times and places has sought to percolate through to us realities about his nature and purposes for us. When and if a person realises that God is doing this, belief is the only response that is right, good and fulfilling. Often, however, those who were supposed to be God's representatives (e.g. priests, prophets, clerks teachers, rulers) claimed that what they said was from God when it was not.

Sometimes people thought they were doing God's will but later reflection showed that they had only partially understood.

The records sometimes make it clear which responses were in line with God's revelation, but sometimes they do not. It is left to us, the readers, to seek our own discernment.

This is a reason why it helps to learn from the discernment that other parts of the Body of Christ (the Church) make of such passages.

Celtic Challenge

Early Celtic Christians (since there were no printed Bibles) had to share transcribed copies of scarce separate books of the Bible. So they had to prioritise the books. They decided that they should start with the four Gospels.

When they read, or had read to them, passages from the Gospels they used their minds, hearts, imaginations and wills. They visualised the risen Christ as being present with them and actually speaking his words to them. They tried to put themselves in the shoes of those who were present with Jesus in the story, but they also put Jesus into their own shoes in the present. Thus the Word of God became a living, flexible reality.

Saint Patrick was called 'the man of the lasting language' because his writings were steeped in Scripture. Ireland became a cradle for the deeper study of Scripture. The Irish schools tended to understand the Bible in its plain, matter-of-fact, meaning, but they discerned four levels at which to understand it: first, the story's meaning for the people written about in the text; second, the meaning this had for generations that followed; third, the moral – what God wants to be different in each of us; and lastly a mystical, symbolic or inner spiritual application.

> The letter kills, the spirit gives life.
>
> *2 Corinthians 3:6*

The Celtic Christians call us to live this truth.

What is the true Church?

Questions

1. The only unity I believe in is unity in the truth. My church is based on the Bible, why waste time with churches that don't believe the Bible?
2. Charismatics have discovered that the Holy Spirit uses people who are not evangelicals, including Roman Catholics, so what does that say to us about church unity?
3. With globalisation, hasn't Christianity got to get its act together? But how?

Response

Both Christians and heretics, including disgraced TV evangelists, have claimed they base their views on the Bible. Martin Luther, who led the Reformers who made the Bible their sole authority, preached anti-Semitic sermons in the name of the Bible. The Jewish 'Bible people' of Jesus' day included self-righteous Pharisees who nit-picked Bible truths but missed the big picture. Jesus told them they made God's word ineffective. He taught that people will know the truth by doing it. Jesus did not teach that God's family on earth consisted of those who claim to base everything on the Bible, it consists of those who do God's will (Luke 8:21)

Celtic Challenge

In the early centuries of Christianity in Britain and Ireland Christians took it for granted that there was one universal Christian Church and that the Bible was the book God had given to it. They also believed that God gave the Holy Spirit to guide Christians as they shared the faith and established new congregations.

They understood that Jesus appointed apostles to carry on the church after his death, and that Jesus, through the Holy Spirit, asked the apostles to appoint leaders to oversee the churches (translated as elders, presbyters, priests, overseers and bishops). They had no concept of independence from the universal Church. If the organised Church fell into bad ways, they challenged the bad ways, as did Columbanus in his letters to two popes in Rome. (See page 53.)

Since then the various strands of Christianity have been torn apart. Today God is calling us to weave together that which is God-given in these separated strands.

Should I do a somersault in church?

Question

I was worshipping Jesus in a church service and felt I should get out of my seat and do a head over heels on the floor! What a strange thing to do. After a while I got up and did it. I found myself a long way from my chair and felt exposed and started to shuffle back. Immediately I felt God was saying 'Don't shuffle back.' Are such impressions from God?

Response

They can be, but they need to be weighed up. Be willing to make a mistake. In your case you were in a church which, as far as you knew, was open to spontaneous movements in worship. If the leadership had asked you not to do such a thing, then you would have respected that.

Celtic Challenge

Many have read about the shy man who thought he could do nothing for God. But the one thing he could do was juggle, so one day he secretly went into a church and juggled in front of the altar. Here is a story of an Irish Christian named Moling who would not accept that songs and smiles were acceptable in church, let alone somersaults – and how his attitude was changed.

Some years after the death of Kevin at Glendalough a very pious monk there, named Moling, used to miss meals in order to pray in the place of worship. Not only did he despise food, he never allowed himself the pleasure of listening to music. Until God sent someone to cheer him up.

One day a young man arrived and asked if he could play his harp to the brothers while they were in the refectory. They welcomed this. Since Moling, who was praying in church, missed this, the young man then went to the church to play. Moling, who was kneeling, did not lift his head, but took from his pocket two balls of wax and stuffed them in his ears.

The young man smiled and continued playing. To Moling's amazement the wax in his ears began to melt. Try as he might to push it back into his ears, it just trickled down under his habit.

At that moment the young man took a stone and started to scrape the harp. Moling found this excruciating sound unbearable. Then the young man threw the stone away and played music so sweet that Moling was filled with a joy greater than he had ever known.

When the harpist had finished playing Moling asked him, 'Are you a devil sent to tempt me or an angel sent to bless me?' 'You must make your own judgement,' the young man replied. 'When I scraped the harp it made the noise of the devil, and when I played it with my fingers it made the sound of an angel. Music, like food and drink, can be an agent of evil or a source of goodness.'

The young man then left. From that day Moling welcomed all musicians to play at the monastery, and he gave up undue fasting, abstaining from food only on those days when everybody fasted. His brothers could not help noticing that from that day onwards he became more gentle and kind, and even acquired a sense of humour.

From Celtic Daily Light, *Ray Simpson (Kevin Mayhew Ltd, 2003)*

Should I give up on the Brethren?

Question

My parents brought me up in a strict Brethren church. I rebelled and got into drugs, drink and violence, and I joined a rock band. One day I met the Holy Spirit in an overwhelming, physical way, and my life has completely changed. But my parents have no place in their scheme of things for the Holy Spirit or for experiencing God with one's feelings. Should I give up on the Brethren?

Response

The Holy Spirit did not give up on you, and I suspect you don't want to give up on the Holy Spirit. So it's really a question of discerning HOW the Holy Spirit wants to help your parents to grow. The Holy Spirit understands your parents' mindset. It is true, as the Bible says, that some people become so hardened, or set in their ways, that they cannot hear God. In that case it may be a question of waiting for the right time; for there are seasons of the soul.

Celtic Challenge

A young Briton, who was named after Samson, the Bible strong man, and who became mighty in works of faith, left his parents' home for ever, as he thought, in order to serve God in an island faith community. However, one wintry day his father was at death's door, and his loved ones urged him to receive Holy Communion before dying. He adamantly refused, he said, until his son Samson should come to him and pray for him, for he knew that his son's prayer, and only his, could restore him to health. A message was brought to Samson's faith community. Samson refused to go, following the letter rather than the spirit of Jesus' words that, unless a person leave their father and mother behind they cannot be his disciple. He walked away from the messengers. However, Samson's spiritual father, Piro, urged him to go 'because God will reward you greatly for sowing spiritual things in the place where human harshness has grown.'

Samson felt weak in faith, and stayed put for another day. Then he asked a brother to accompany him in prayer. When they arrived Samson's father asked everyone else to leave, confessed a major sin, and dedicated his life to God. His wife supported him, saying, 'Let not only me and you serve God, but let our whole family be linked together in God's service and let all that is ours become wholly God's.'

This led to all Samson's five brothers and his sister, as well as both his parents, making vows of full-time service for God. The result was that Samson's father was healed, they went on faith-sharing trips together, and the different members of the family planted churches in new places.

What should I do if my church turns people off?

Question

I live on a city council estate. Most of my neighbours choose not to read. Yet what does the local church offer? Cultural imperialism! They expect people to use hymn-books, sit in pews and behave in a way that is totally alien to them. Should I give up on the church? If so, what should I do about my non-Christian neighbours?

Response

First, get clear that your particular church is an aberration. It is not a model of a Christian church, that is, a church that represents Christ to the people. In the Celtic way you plant an expression of Christ in the natural social patterns of the people.

Second, if you have a relationship with people who lead churches in your area, talk to them about what you feel, and find out if others think the same way as you.

Celtic Challenge

Follow the example of Celtic church planters. Think about the Gospel-neutral or Gospel-friendly patterns in your area: where people socialise, drink, make music, play, keep fit, enjoy sport, have karaokes. Pray that you will find one or two others who share your vision. Meet with them in one of those places. And as folk join you, keep good relationships with your middle-class church nearby!

When does a church become a cult?

Question

My husband has joined a new church movement. They want to possess him.

He is no longer a free man. They don't like me because I won't be told what I must do. I admit his morals have improved, but he no longer thinks his own thoughts or takes me seriously. Are they a cult? Should I leave him, join them or what?

Response

A UK Government agency has issued an excellent report on the nature of cults. Here are six tests which can help a church to avoid becoming a cult:

1. Maintain relationships with the wider church.
2. The leaders are accountable to an independent person or group that is outside their local set-up.
3. Members are allowed to have a spiritual mentor or soul friend who is not a member of that church.
4. Leaders provide transparent accounts of their money.
5. A spirit of hospitality welcomes people who do not join – there is not a 'them' and 'us' mentality.

6. There are opportunities for members to disagree and be listened to.

Often a person is drawn to a 'heavy shepherding' church because they are insecure. Don't make your husband more insecure by berating him: love him and gently introduce him to people, films, books and sources wider than those of his church. If I were you I would use every opportunity, such as holidays, education and leisure programmes to jointly make links with Christians of different backgrounds. Give the all-pervading Holy Spirit a chance.

Celtic Challenge

> For all we Irish . . . are disciples of Saints Peter and Paul and of all the disciples who wrote the sacred canon (of Scripture) by the Holy Spirit. We accept nothing outside the evangelical and apostolic teaching. None of us was a heretic . . . no one a schismatic . . .
>
> *Columbanus in a letter to Boniface, leader of the church in Rome, 613.*

> We ask . . . that we may be able to live among (the churches of Gaul) with the peace of church unity. This what the holy forefathers, Polycarp and Anicetus, taught – to live without offence to the Faith – indeed, perservering in perfect love – each retaining what he has received and 'remain within your calling.'
>
> *Columbanus in a letter to the new leader of the church in Rome 604 or 607.*

> Be many sided and adaptable to the direction of those who obey you with faith and love.
>
> *Columbanus' letter to the leader of the monks at Luxeuil, 610.*

Does the future have a church?

Question

I have felt the Lord asking me this question: 'Does the future have a church?' (rather than 'does the church have a future?'). I firmly believe that what we have now will not last, and I look forward to a model of church that will be so completely different from what we see now that it will be unrecognisable. I sense people are looking for a church that talks about real life issues – like marriage, divorce, singleness, sex . . . When was the last time you heard a sermon on sex, where real life issues were spoken of such as debt, vocation, living with the husband/wife who is this and who is that, the homeless, drug addiction, pornography, the internet, gambling, redundancy? Our streets, work places and shopping malls are full of people asking these very questions, yet no one will listen or walk with these folks. I am still working through these many ideas, and still I wait and listen because I don't have the answer.

Response

I believe you are right to look forward to a church that is very different, and that many of the externals of what we have now will not last. Indeed, your inference that your list of topics would be best dealt with in sermons may itself be part of the old church framework that needs to go.

I see church as being what the members do during the week – caring, mentoring, celebrating, praying, reaching out, working. Sunday is a good day to touch base. They can come and go and meet up as they please on that day.

They may have some worship if they wish, but a sermon-centred service is not the focus.

There is so much pain, and complexity, and so many individual factors at work in these issues that they are best dealt with in the context of the spiritual formation of individuals and friendship groups.

Church is the place where people come to chill out, to off-load, to worship, to choose from a menu.

Celtic Challenge

Post-modern churches are emerging that resonate at a deep level with the experience of the early Celtic faith communities in these islands. At the same time that there is a decline in the 'one-shape-fits-all' type of church, there is a mushrooming of Christian projects, culture-friendly church plants and networks. which can become 'villages of God'. These seven-day-a-week villages of God typically include several of these features:

* Daily corporate prayer
* Eating places – e.g. cafes
* Accommodation units – e.g. hostel, B&B, on-site units for members
* Learning courses – resource centre
* Work and creative arts projects
* Sacred space
* Mentors and counsellors
* Allotments, gardens or another earth-friendly link

* Facilities for all or most ages
* Social entertainment

The village of God is like a wheel with spokes that reach into the hub-places of society. The spoke takes the form of a supportive presence WITHIN the cultural pattern of the hub. The hubs may include:

* School
* Health centre
* Supermarket
* Pub
* Sports teams
* Fitness centre
* Community centre
* Bingo club
* Uniformed organisations
* Police
* Social services
* Local media
* Centres of other religions
* Places where disaffected groups hang out
* Night clubs
* The homeless

Their values are likely to include:

* Respect for life
* Seeing Christ in the face of the other person
* Unity in diversity
* Transparency

These values echo those expressed in the New Testament symbolism of the human body, each of whose parts honours and works with the others, under the leadership of the Head, who is Christ.

What's wrong with evangelism?

Question

Evangelism has got a bad name these days. What's wrong with it?

Response

A better question is 'What's right with evangelism?' Here is an example of evangelism from inside a culture.

Celtic Challenge

Patrick, early evangelist of northern Ireland, was a teenage Briton and a nominal Christian who was kidnapped by an Irish raider and put to labour as a slave in his Slemish fields in County Antrim. There he turned to God with all his heart, and after six years escaped by boat in obedience to a vision. He trained as a missionary, was ordained on the continent, and returned to his beloved British home. But there he received another vision: the Irish people, who had so few Christians, were calling him to bring Christ to them.

So he came with a faith-sharing team. He faced huge odds but, because he had been immersed for six years both in the life of the land and of the Holy Spirit, he had discerned certain Gospel-friendly 'handles' which he would seize with flair and turn to God's advantage.

The leading druid advisors of Ireland's High King, Loiguire (Dublin's main ferry is named after him), had foretold the coming of a foreign way of life which would replace their own religion. Ireland was ripe for something new. Patrick presented Christianity as the fulfilment of the prophecies of the wisest indigenous advisors.

Patrick could discern the spirit of people who were predisposed to goodness and who would therefore welcome him and his message. Patrick's group disembarked at Strangford Lough and walked inland to rest. There the swineherd of a naturally good pagan named Dicu discovered them, and brought them to Dicu who lived in the area. Dicu, thinking they were bandits, resolved to kill them, but when he saw Patrick's face he instantly recognised goodness and changed his mind. Patrick, following Jesus' advice to missioners to stay in homes where they were made welcome, postponed his plans and stayed several days with Dicu. Dicu was discipled, baptised and became one of a praying back-up force for Patrick's mission. Indeed, one of the first churches of Ireland was established there at Strangford Lough and the Faith spread from there. The best foundation for any mission is to spend time with God discerning who are the naturally good people who will welcome 'the genuine article' when they meet it.

Is TULIP crap?

Question

I enrolled at a conservative evangelical theological college and had a shock. In my country the words 'conservative' and 'evangelical' mean something quite different and more positive. In the first term they taught the five points of Calvinism under the heading T.U.L.I.P. These don't fit my experience or my understanding of the Bible. To be frank, I think they are crap. I'd never want to believe in a God like they present. Should I stick it out, argue it out, or get out?

Response

Roger Forster, founder of the Icthus church network in the UK, has argued it out with Paul Marston in his book *God's Strategy in Human History* (Wipf & Stock Publishers: Eugene, Oregon). Let's take the five points:

> **T**otal Depravity
> (also known as Total Inability and Original Sin);
>
> **U**nconditional Election
> (the majority, who are shut out of God's election,
> have no choice in the matter);
>
> **L**imited Atonement (also known as Particular Atonement
> – Jesus died only for the elect);

Irresistible Grace (when God calls his elect into salvation, they cannot resist and they have no choice);

Perseverance of the Saints (also known as Once Saved Always Saved – even if you become a Satan worshipper or a mass terrorist).

The horrible thing about presenting the wonder of God's work in this way is that it reduces it to mental statements that tie people up in knots. Steve Chalke* hit the headlines on this. He said that a God who gets angry at humans and then takes it out on his own Son by killing him is the equivalent of a cosmic child abuser.

Celtic Challenge

Total Depravity: The Celtic author and former Warden of Iona Abbey, Philip Newell, contrasts the Celtic view with the Mediterranean view which Augustine introduced and Calvin developed further. In the Celtic view we do not define ourselves by the ugliness of our failings as much as by the beauty of our origins in God. These have been distorted but not destroyed by sin. Sin is pervasive and real, but it is not the essence of who we are.

Unconditional Election: Fatalism ('what will be, will be, so why bother to right wrongs or reach out to those who have lost their way'), which many who pursue astrology fall prey to, is not Christian. Jesus likens his own attitude to that of a shepherd who goes on seeking until he finds the last lost sheep, and after his death Jesus sought to win trapped

---

*Steve Chalke is a TV presenter and Director of *Faithworks*, an organisation that sponsors activities which witness to Jesus through both words and social action.

spirits of the departed to God (1 Peter 3:19). Why do you think Jesus never wasted one breath talking about 'unconditional election'?

Limited Atonement: Cuthbert (from Melrose, seventh century) strove to convert people from miles around from their foolish ways. They confessed their darkest secrets to him. He made a point of searching out people in steep, rugged places that others would not visit because of their squalor. To him, it was a labour of love. He was so keen that sometimes he would live rough for weeks with the hill folk, calling them heavenwards by his example.

Irresistible Grace: Biblical writers tell people 'do not harden your hearts as your predecessors did' (e.g. Psalm 95:8). Jesus says: 'If you forgive others the wrongs they have done to you, your Father in heaven will also forgive you. But if you do not forgive others, then your Father in heaven will not forgive the wrongs you have done' (Matthew 6:14-15). The apostle Peter said, 'Whoever does what is right is acceptable to God' (Acts 10:34-35).

> We alone have the capacity to distinguish between good and evil, right and wrong. This means that our actions need not be compulsions, we do not have to be swayed by our immediate wants and desires, as are the animals. Instead, we can make choices. Day by day, hour by hour, we have to make decisions. In each decision we can choose either good or evil. This freedom to choose makes us like God. If we choose evil, that freedom becomes a curse. If we choose good, it becomes our greatest blessing.
>
> *Pelagius – sixth-century Celtic holy man and teacher.*

Perseverance of the saints: Who will be saved? Not the one who says 'Lord', but the one who shows mercy (Matthew 25).

> Columba, leader of the sixth-century faith community on the Scottish island of Iona, heard that a colleague planned to bring his friend to stay with the community. 'We cannot welcome this fellow here', said the prophetic Columba, 'for he has committed a bestial sin.' At the ferry, however, the man confessed his sin and agreed to undergo spiritual discipline. One of Columba's aides then pressed Columba to relent, and accept him, and quoted Scriptures to support this advice. 'This man has killed his brother and debauched his own mother,' said Columba. The man agreed to spend twelve years away from his own country under discipline. After he left, Columba informed his people: 'This man is a son of perdition who will not carry out the discipline. Before long he will go back to Ireland where he will die at the hands of enemies.'
>
> Life of Columba, *Book 1, chapter 22, by Adomán of Iona, translated by Richard Sharpe (Penguin 1995)*

Is 24-7 a flash in the pan?

Question

The 24-7 Movement to keep prayer going every hour of a week is exciting and is catching on all over the place. But won't it be a flash in the pan?*

Response

Enthusiasm without a plan leads to burn-out. The boiler house movement is trying to create round-the-clock prayer all through the year ('boiler houses' are prayer and caring centres similarly open all the time). This has created a problem: once people who are out of work, on drugs or homeless know that nice praying people will always be around in a certain place, they make a bee-line for it. Then socialising takes over from the prayer if you are not careful. But if we can let the Holy Spirit guide us into a God-given framework which provides spaces for the different elements that are needed for a rounded, prayerful community witness, then it will not be a flash in the pan, but a constantly burning fire.

---

* 24-7 Prayer is an international and interdenominational prayer and mission movement, founded by Pete Greig and profiled in *Red Moon Rising* by Pete Greig and Dave Roberts (Kingsway, 2004). In forty-six countries people are praying 24 hours a day, 7 days a week, with as many as 20 prayer rooms running concurrently. *www.24-7prayer.com*

Celtic Challenge

Bangor, in Northern Ireland, was typical of the early Irish faith communities. Over 3,000 Christians devoted themselves to the singing of Perennial Praise, based on the form of worship in the Tabernacle of King David. This place later became known as Bangor Mor, The Great High Choir. Their praise book, the Bangor Antiphonary, which is preserved in the Ambrosian Library, Milan, says, 'Let the many keep awake in community on a third of the nights in the year in order to read aloud from the Book and to expound judgement and to sing blessings all together.' Bernard of Clairvaux called this place The Valley of Angels.

The Antiphonary contains hymns, prayers and festal shouts for use alongside the Bible and the Book of Psalms.

Monasteries such as Bangor had a routine framework of Psalms, canticles, prayers, creeds, responses and Bible readings. These varied from season to season and from monastery to monastery; each had a local flavour. We learn of a group of young monks who were so keen to keep up a ceaseless round of praise that they asked permission to sing Psalm 119, the longest Psalm by far, seven times each day! Most worshippers had no books. They said prayers and festal shouts 'from the gut'.

Worship in Celtic churches was in the context of community. Worshippers would have time to eat and talk together as part of a total event, they would not be pew sitters who returned to separate lives without interaction. Visitors knew there were periods for work, silence, corporate prayer, study, celebration, eating. They observed these boundaries. Thus people did not suffer burn-out or dependency. Outside some of these faith communities a fire was kept alight for a thousand years.

How do I cope with liberal Christians who hit back?

Question

I am a conservative evangelical Christian leader. I speak out against liberal stances in the church. My church withdraws its financial contribution to any Christian body that refuses to stand with us. Now, I am being persecuted by liberal Christians, and am on medication for stress. What should I do?

Response

The prophet Elijah suffered persecution followed by exhaustion as a result of taking a stand. He went into retreat. I recommend you to take sick leave and do the same. Once Elijah was out of his normal religious framework, God was able to speak to him through the elements. Why not give time to being alone with God in the elements?

Celtic Challenge

Learn to view other Christians not as strangers, but as fellow pilgrims.

> 'What then are you, human life?
>
> You are the road to life, not life itself.

You are a real road but not a level one,
Long for some, short for others,
Broad for some, narrow for others,
Joyful for some, sad for others.
For all alike, fleeting and irrevocable.
A road is what you are, a road,
But you are not clear to all.
Many see you
And few understand you to be a road.
For you are so wily and enticing
That few know you are a road.

Therefore you are to be questioned
But not believed and given bail.
You are to be traversed but not inhabited . . .

For no one dwells on a road, but travels it
So that those who walk upon the road
May dwell in their homeland.'

From Columbanus in his own Words*, Tomás Ó Fraich (Veritas 1974)*

Can a Bible Christian be a mystic?

Question

I was told that mystics lead you astray because they imagine things that are not in the Bible. Can a Bible Christian be a mystic?

Response

The Bible records many mystical experiences, from Jacob seeing a ladder going into heaven to the apostle Paul knowing someone (probably himself) who was being caught up into the seventh heaven.

You could hardly get more biblical Christians than the Presbyterians of the Hebridean Isle of Lewis. Yet in the nineteenth century, hundreds of Presbyterian men went into the woods to seek God. They had mystical experiences, and then moved through the towns and villages. Revival broke out.

Celtic Challenge

Ita's parents were Christians who named her Deidre, but her name was changed to Ita, which means 'thirst', because of her extraordinary thirst for Divine love. Even as a child she had mystical experiences. One night she dreamt that an angel offered her three precious stones, explaining that these represented the Father, the Son, and the Holy Spirit and that 'always in your sleep and vigils, the angels of God and holy visions will come to you, for you are a temple of God in body and soul.'

Once her father released her to her adult ministry, Ita began to fast, pray and listen so as to discern the meaning of her life. The Holy Spirit gave her discernment of spirits in herself and in others. She was led to Killeedy, where other women joined her and she gave spiritual counsel to both women and men.

Once, one of Ita's nuns, who was in a convent some distance away, committed fornication, but kept it secret. Ita summoned her, told her exactly when and where she had transgressed, and urged her to guard her virginity. This prophetic word brought a change of heart; the nun willingly undertook exercises to build up her ability to master sexual temptations, and thereafter succeeded in living a pure life.

Ita's discernment was possible because she often retreated to the solitude of her hut, where it was said the company of heaven was so near that she became the nursemaid of Christ.

One of her disciples once asked her what was the secret of her gifts of discernment, healing and her mystical experiences of God. Ita put it down to regular meditation since her childhood, and her constant inviting in of the Three Persons of the Trinity. She died in 569 and was known as a foster mother of Ireland's Christians.

Can you follow Jesus while you've got an overdraft?

Question

'Sell your possessions and follow me,' (Mark 10:21) said Jesus. Yes, I'd like to, but not only do I not have many possessions, I have a huge student loan and a bank overdraft – I can't just walk away from those can I?

Response

Well, actually, if you followed a calling that brought low pay you would not have to pay your student loan back. Your overdraft is different. The best way to approach that is to make a plan.

Question

What kind of a plan?

Response

I know someone who stopped buying bottled drinks and processed food: they stuck to simple home-made food and drink. They put the money they saved into a loan-repayment fund. In addition, they got a Saturday job and vacation jobs and saved a lot by having a stay-at-home but creative holiday. They got a kick out of meeting their weekly repayment target.

Once you've got a working plan, the question to ask is: what is Christ calling me to do? The guy Jesus told to sell his possessions was rich and addicted to money.

So the point here is: Place everything you have into Jesus' hands and be willing for him to show you what to do with it.

If you are not addicted to money Jesus might guide you to become a brilliant business entrepreneur. Unlikely, but possible.

The important thing is to find out what Jesus has made you to be – what are your convictions, creativities – where does your compassion point you to? And your talents?

You can follow Jesus by trying things out in order to discover the answer. We follow Jesus by trying to think, feel, speak and act as he would if he were in your situation.

Celtic Challenge

> Shall I abandon, O King of Mysteries, the soft comforts of home? Shall I turn my back on my native land, and my face towards the sea?
>
> Shall I put myself wholly at the mercy of God, without silver, without a horse, without fame and honour? Shall I throw myself wholly on the King of kings, without a sword and shield, without food and drink, without a bed to lie on?
>
> Shall I say farewell to my beautiful land, placing myself under Christ's yoke? Shall I pour out my heart to him, confessing my manifold sins and begging forgiveness, tears running down my cheeks?

Shall I leave the prints of my knees on the sandy beach, a record of my final prayer in my native land? Shall I then suffer every kind of wound that the sea can inflict?

Shall I take my tiny coracle across the wide, sparkling ocean? O King of the Glorious heaven, shall I go of my own choice upon the sea?

O Christ, will you help me on the wild waves?

An early Irish prayer.

Would you pray to a saint?

Question

Would you pray to a saint? If so, why?

Response

I would never pray to a saint because I thought I could not pray direct to God through Christ. Nor because I wanted something that I would not want to bother God with. Least of all because I wanted something selfish and I might twist the arm of a saint while God wasn't looking!

I do, however, ask other Christians to pray for things. I do this, even though I know that God can answer my prayers directly without taking notice of their prayers. I do this because the Bible tells us to pray for one another (James 5:16). It seems clear that God intends a world where we are interdependent. God likes community. We are meant to care for one another, to know one another, and to pray for one another.

I do not believe that when a Christian dies (s)he is extinguished. The Bible teaches that dead Christians are alive, not in a physical body, but in Christ. Dead Christians are around us like a cloud of witnesses (Hebrews 12:1). Witnesses are alive, aware, present. So it would be unnatural and unchristian to treat them as if they could not continue as part of the praying community. The universal Body of Christ includes those on earth and in heaven (see Ephesians 1:21-23).

Question

In what circumstances would you pray to a saint?

Response

The deepest, continual prayer of my heart is to God. Examples of my most frequent prayers are 'Father, your kingdom come', 'Jesus, have mercy upon me', and 'Spirit, renew us'. So I basically pray to the Trinity. I am aware that the Trinity is the source of a vast community. So the more aware I am of the Trinity, the more aware I become of this community. That is why a favourite Bible name for God is 'The Lord of hosts'.

Sometimes, God brings an awareness of a particular member of his community.

This may be because I am in a place where a saint lived – so Francis came especially to my mind when I was in Assisi. In many traditional churches you see Christ on the cross in the middle of the altar, and his mother Mary on his right, and his dearest friend John, on his left. They were a spiritual family. Sometimes I pray: 'Jesus, Mary and John, embrace this lonely, lost person for whom I pray, and let them know they are part of your family, too.' Often it is because I am in need, or the folk for whom I intercede are in need, of a quality I associate with a particular saint.

Celtic Challenge

I am a member of The Community of Aidan and Hilda. Aidan and Hilda pioneered the Irish Mission to the English in the seventh century. I believe God guided the founders of this new task-force of Christians to name itself after these two saints and for a reason. They represent a spirituality that God wants to foster today. I associate Aidan with the sort of Christian who gets off their high horse and enters into the world of the other person, without any feeling of threat; someone who is true, just, gentle and who lives the presence of Christ so fully that many others want to follow Christ in simplicity of life. I associate Hilda with the fostering of callings and wisdom. So sometimes I include them in my chats with God: 'Aidan, I know you resisted the temptation to be a superstar or to push people into the right ways. Help me to hold back in this situation. Stop me from mucking everything up. Help me to learn from your example. So help me God.' Or, 'Hilda, help this person to understand what you understood, may they be another of your spiritual children – assuming you approve, Jesus.'

Should Christians be on celebrity TV?

Question

A Christian mate dared us to apply to go on a reality TV programme. He says he gets a kick out of mixing with celebrities or becoming an overnight celebrity, and Christians should get in there. Should we?

Response

Take a look at Andy Warhol's art. It is a projection of everything that can be bought and sold – the fleeting symbols we are addicted to. It defines our culture of celebrity, sex, boredom, money, mass production and violence. He saw that fame and beauty were the compensatory pleasures for a population consumed with fear and paranoia.

So we have a choice. We are free to try for celebrity TV, and we are free to be true to ourselves. The first has a short term 'up' and a long term 'down' – because the surface ego stuff disintegrates and actual reality takes over. The second has a long term 'up'.

Celtic Challenge

Chad could have been a bit of a seventh-century celebrity. He was top in his class at the first school of English boys in Lindisfarne, and was chosen to do further education in Ireland. He was made bishop of the Northumbrians. He could have had the trappings of status and power – such as a royal horse for his transport. He chose instead to walk everywhere, dress simply and be one of the people. A prelate named Wilfred, who was in love with celebrity culture, managed to get Chad ousted. This humble man said, 'I never thought I was worthy to be a bishop in the first place, so that's fine by me.' The Archbishop of Canterbury was so impressed by Chad's freedom from chasing after status that he offered him another post as bishop of a large slice of middle England, and he insisted that Chad ride a horse, personally lifting him up into the saddle.

Jesus noticed how guests were taking the best
places at a banquet, so he told this story:
When someone invites you to a wedding banquet
do not sit down on the top table.
Someone more important than you might have a
place reserved for them,
and when your host explains this to you you will
be embarrassed.
It is better to sit at the lowest place, so that the
host will say 'Come to a better place.'
Everyone who tries to be the greatest will be
brought low;
everyone who humbles themselves will be made
great.

Luke 14:7-11

Is God in mobile phones or in silence?

Question

The mobile phone is already out of date – the technological revolution means we can be connected all the time. When I was young I thought this was great. As I've got older the pace of change has been getting quicker and quicker and it makes me feel insecure and uncertain. I know change is inevitable but I can't feel comfortable in this restless world. Is God in the change or in the stillness?

Response

God's thoughts are not your thoughts (Isaiah 55:8); they are much faster than mobile phones and much deeper than the deepest stillness.

If everyone who used a mobile phone or texted messages had equilibrium in their souls, the world would be filling out with more harmony, creativity, love and understanding. Modern technology is a God-given opportunity: it becomes a blessing or a curse according to how it is used.

I know churches that ban mobile phones during services. I know another church in which everyone has a mobile phone and texts the sermon to friends while it is being preached.

So the real issue is: which comes first, the cart or the horse? The first thing to get right is relationship with God, that deep inner attentiveness that enables us to handle tasks and technology in a godly way. In order to develop this quality we do need to create spaces when we abstain from mobile phones etc. It is a modern form of fasting. It can be a challenge and fun to fast in this way.

Celtic Challenge

I was inspired to learn of a monk who left his monastery, not because he was giving up on God, but because, in the time of still reflection that the monastery provided for him he realised he had a vocation to the fast-moving world of business. I like to think that in the high-pressure atmosphere of the city boardroom he was able to maintain inner calm and refrain from frenetic actions, because his schooling in the disciplines of meditation enabled him to work from stillness, rather than vice versa.

> I pledge to maximise CD, audio cassette, phone and recording facilities in my car, home, office and travelling in order to communicate, learn and use my talents most creatively, as inspired by God. I also pledge to abstain from these for three periods each year, and between Night Prayer and breakfast daily, and to keep silence during these periods when possible.
>
> *The Personal Rule of a member of The Community of Aidan and Hilda.*

What do you think of white witches?

Question

What do you think of white witches? I have been told that 'the baddies' are Christians who demonised wise women and killed them as witches in the Middle Ages, and that modern white witches are 'the goodies' who are into healing and doing good.

Response

Witches use magic, be it black or white. Magic is the use of natural, psychic or spirit forces to influence the course of events in a person or place.

Modern white witches may offer psychic readings, aura cleansings or spell kits.

Witch hunting by Christians was a wrong and un-Christ-like way to address the fears and mind-control that were part of medieval witchcraft.

Jesus told his friends, 'Whoever is not against us is for us' (Mark 9:40). If a white witch is friendly towards you and Jesus, I would foster that friendship in the hope that her understanding of Jesus will grow.

Some people are more psychically aware than others. If they do a psychic reading they may pick up psychic tendencies in the client, but they will also project on to these their own psychic material and psychic patterns based on other clients. These can be mistaken. More important, they feed fear or curiosity about the future, and, even if the witch means them well, do not put the client in touch with the Source of healing and wholeness.

God certainly wants to use the wisdom of psychically aware people. The best way is for such a person to consecrate their insight to Christ, purify their psyche in continual prayer and Scripture meditation, release each person from their desire to control, and point them to the One who alone knows their end from their beginning.

Such people can make good anamcharas or soul friends.

Celtic Challenge

If you have a white witch friend whose advice you value, why not invite her to say this prayer with you?

> I arise today in the aura of the All-Good God
> Who sees and knows all
> The Birther who formed me
> The Redeemer who heals me
> The Spirit who leads me.
>
> For my shield this day I invite:
> Strong power of the angels
> In the glorious company of the holy and risen ones.
>
> For my shield this day I invite
> Heaven's might
> Sun's brightness
> Moon's whiteness
> Fire's glory
> Lightning's swiftness

Wind's wildness
Ocean's depth
Earth's solidity.

For my shield this day I invite
God's strength to direct me
God's wisdom to guide me.

Around me I gather these forces to save me from
Dark powers that assail me
And from false prophesyings
Spells and advice that pull me away from You.

Christ beside me, Christ before me,
Christ behind me, Christ within me;
Christ beneath me, Christ above me,
Christ in eye of all who see me.

For my shield this day I invite:
A mighty power;
The Holy Trinity!
Affirming Threeness,
Confessing Oneness,
In the making of all through love.

Echoes St Patrick's Breastplate.

What now for streetwise Pentecostals?

Questions

1. I am a third generation Pentecostal, and I am in the same church as my parents and grandparents. My generation of Pentecostals is streetwise. We don't go for hype, routine ranting and false claims of miracles. We could easily get cynical. We need to hold on to something solid. What?
2. I choose to be in a charismatic church. But the charismatic flow can easily become shallow. What could give me an anchor?

Response

Living worship combines depth, balance and authenticity as well as room for spontaneity. There is nothing wrong with structure; it is not unspiritual or legalistic. Otherwise, why did God make the world? There is structure in every atom. What we need is a living, organic structure.

Celtic Challenge

In contemporary Celtic-style worship there is a restoration of elements of worship which, creatively combined, make for wholeness. Jews, such as Daniel, prayed three times a day in the rhythm of the sun's rising, zenith and setting – Celtic worship restores our primal, instinctive awareness of God in creation. Scriptures are memorised and recited: repetition and familiarity can be primal, too. Yet there is sensitivity and awareness of the seasons of nature and of the soul. Thus tears, silence and lament can be as valid as tongues, shouts and laughter. There is a time for contemplation. Churches seek to be like a large household with different rooms. These rooms suit people of different temperaments and in different stages of life. In these churches people can come and go, and have space for themselves. Also, a church can have a season without their routine style of worship. The *Celtic Prayer Book* series, published by Kevin Mayhew Ltd, provides examples of worship material that has these ingredients, together with creative activities.

Global warming – catastrophe or opportunity?

Question

Some evangelicals say that the increase in earthquakes and hurricanes is a sign that the end of the world is imminent, when God will fold up the earth and skies in fire as suggested in 2 Peter 3:10; so Christians should focus their energies on saving souls before this happens. Other Christians say these catastrophes are made worse by global warming caused by humans, and Christians should focus their energies on changing our personal and national lifestyles. Some people in the Christian Right in the USA say these disasters are merely natural cycles and we should focus our energies on research that fixes these things. Who is right?

Response

You are mixing different issues here. It is not 'either-or' but 'both-and'. Jesus said there will always be earthquakes and suchlike on earth (Matthew 24:7). The Bible also teaches that God speaks to us through things that happen in nature, e.g. Psalm 18:6-15. Jesus likens the planet to a vineyard that his people are meant to tend with care (Luke 20:9-16).

In western societies progress is measured by the rate of

energy consumption and acquisition of material goods. The biblical teaching given to God's people during and after Moses' time was that progress is measured by the degree of well-being in relationship to the environment, neighbours and to God. In order to sustain this quality of life limits on consumption and working hours were needed, which renewed both the land and the people who lived on it.

Deep ecology recognises that the flourishing of both human and non-human life has intrinsic value and that the ecosphere is inter-related. This insight should be obvious to Christians whose eyes are open, since we believe that the Source of creation (God) has also entered into it in order to draw the whole created order into harmony with God (Colossians 1:15-20).

Celtic Challenge

Chad (a monk trained in Lindisfarne who died in 672) was greatly filled with the fear of the Lord and was mindful of his last end in all he did. If a high wind arose, he would immediately stop whatever he was doing and pray God to have mercy on the human race. If the wind became a gale he would lie prostrate in earnest prayer. If there was a violent storm, lightning or thunder he would go to the church and devote himself to prayers and psalms until it passed.

When people asked him why he did this he replied: 'Have you not read "The Lord also thundered in the heavens and the Most High gave voice. Yes, the Most High sent arrows and scattered the people, shot out lightnings and discomforted them?" For the Lord moves the air, raises the winds, hurls the inhabitants to revere him, to remind them of future judgement in order to scatter their pride and confound their presumption. The Lord does this by calling to their minds the time when he will come in clouds in great power and majesty to judge the living and the dead, while the heavens and the earth are aflame.'

Chad concluded, 'And so we ought to respond to God's heavenly warning with due fear and love, so that as often as he disturbs the sky and raises his hand as if about to strike, yet spares us still, we should implore his mercy, examining our consciences, turning from our sins, and thereafter behaving with such care so that we do not deserve to be struck down.'

Leader	This we know, the earth does not belong to us.
All	We belong to the earth.
Leader	This we know, all things are connected,
All	Like the blood that unites one family.
Leader	This we know, we did not weave the web of life
All	We are merely a strand in it.
Leader	This we know, whatever we do to the web,
All	We do to ourselves.
Leader	Let us give thanks for the gift of creation.
All	Let us give thanks that all things hold together in Christ.

From 'Morning Prayer for Autumn' in Healing the Land, *volume 3 of the* Celtic Prayer Book *(Kevin Mayhew Ltd)*

Tsunamis and the pain question

Question

I am pulled apart by Christians who give their spin on the pain question – especially after the tsunami that hit Asia at the end of 2004. One lot of Christians say God has no place for suffering: suffering is God's judgement on people and nations; if someone remains in pain after Christians pray for them it is because they lack faith. Another lot say we should welcome suffering, like Jesus did on the cross: no pain, no gain. What do you think?

Answer

Jesus said, 'The sun and rain fall on good and bad alike.' So one person may have a life of sunshine, and another may have unbearable pain, and this may be nothing to do with their faith or lack of it.

The world God has created has the possibility of suffering built in to it. Think of humanity as a body, and every person as a member of that body. Even if one member suffers badly, it remains connected to the rest of the body. Other members of the body feel it. If one part suffers, all suffer. Likewise, love and comfort flow from parts that do not suffer to the part that does.

Christians tie much of their thinking about God to things such as blessing, protection, provision, gift. God shows us his loving kindness in these things. He is our Benefactor. The danger is that we then subtly pervert the way God is by tying God to our human desire that 'everything in the garden be rosy'.

Celtic Challenge

If Christianity is to hold our world, Christians need to accept the world and God as they are, not as we would like them to be. We need to accept that the earth is subject to, not faults but a structural basis that includes the movement of its crust. To live in a wonderful universe is to be subject to its potential dangers. The universe is ALIVE, active, evolving. It is not 'safe' in the sense of a security guarantee we might demand of an insurance company.

The view that it should be 'safe' grows out of the false mindset that now governs almost every section of our society. Schools no longer dare organise adventure trips lest a parent sues them for any mishap. Social workers and therapists dare not let people in crisis journey through their pain; they dull the symptoms and bury the roots lest they lose their job in the event that something goes wrong. Our immune systems are not fully exercised and asthma increases because of our addiction to unnatural hygiene.

Celtic Christian spirituality recognises that there is an element of wildness in the planet and in the person, and that if we avoid journeying into this wildness we do not fully live. We acknowledge that the earth is not simply a resource for human domination; that God does not show his love by removing danger from our lives, but by the gift of himself in all circumstances – in delights, dangers and death.

God has not provided a nest for us to enjoy a quiet life. He calls us to live as part of a universal human body, so that when one member suffers we, too, suffer. We can recognise God's love in creation by the desire he puts in us to gather together when disaster scatters people, and to come alongside those who suffer.

Why waste time on this world?

Question

People at my church make me feel guilty if I get involved in anything that is not spiritual, even if it is giving practical help to others. They say Jesus might come again any minute, so our time should go into saving souls. Even if I got a first in my university degree course, or won an Olympic gold medal, they would not bother to come to the celebration: they would think those things were worthless compared to bringing one soul to Christ. This makes me feel constricted – almost a prisoner of their point of view. What should I do?

Response

According to the Acts of the Apostles, the Christians in Jerusalem chose people who were full of the Holy Spirit to focus, not on evangelism, but on practical caring for the needy – widows with no help from a welfare state (Acts 6:1-6). This released others to evangelise. They realised that both social care and evangelism were important.

Celtic Challenge

The members of David's sixth-century faith community in Wales ploughed the land daily with yokes on their shoulders, praying as they worked in silence. With their own efforts they provided for all the needs of the community and for many needy people in the region around. If old or tired visitors came, they would cook them appetising meals, even though they themselves had only one cooked meal a day. They offered hospitality to many. It was said that at David's death 'kings mourned him as a judge, the older people as a brother, the younger as a father.' The idea was to plant colonies of heaven on earth. This is in line with Jesus' request that we pray 'Your kingdom come on earth, as it is in heaven.' By actually modelling something of heaven on earth in the reality of the different aspects of life, more people were turned to God than by any amount of preaching that was not backed up by a model.

Can we campaign against poverty without being patronising?

Question

Jesus said we will always have the poor with us. Is wiping off third world debt a good thing – won't they just want more? If I join the Make Poverty History Campaign won't it be patronising?

Answer

Jesus did not say 'in that case you need do nothing'. He actually said that those who get entry to God's kingdom will be those who serve the poor (Matthew 25:31-46).

I know Christians who work in aid organisations. They tell me that some African leaders take aid money to enrich themselves and their families; they do not care if millions of their people starve. What do I learn from this? That aid needs to be twin-track.

Our political leaders in the West are like people who have one eye open and one eye shut. We need to export values, character, spirituality, that motivates a new generation to be absolutely honest, to get involved, to live simply, to see through the chain by which aid reaches the person in the village who needs it.

Celtic Challenge

A farmer named Colman always received Columba and his monks with great generosity even though he was poor. Columba gave a prophetic blessing that Colman's stock of cattle would increase from five to one hundred and five and his children would likewise prosper. This was fulfilled, but a bigwig named Ioan took to plundering Colman's farm and shipping off its produce. One day Columba caught and confronted Ioan, who mocked Columba. So Columba waded in to the water and raised both hands to heaven as the boat sailed off. He returned to his companions and prophesied: 'This wretched man who has despised Christ in his servants will never return to this bay. Before sun sets they will be killed in a storm.'

Both prophesies came true. Columba saw issues clearly and took responsibility to see that the poor were aided and that the corrupt did not get away with things.

Are eco-Christians middle-class freaks?

Question

Christians in middle-class areas push ecology, and Christians in rural areas go on about creation, but they are divorced from the poor in sink estates. So why should people in inner cities care about all this?

Response

Celtic Christians connect with the poor with one hand and with creation with the other – and they hold Christ, who is in the poor and in the creation, in their hearts at all times.

The lack of interest that many people in socially deprived areas show towards the environment is linked to low self-esteem. If they think that they, the peak of creation, are rubbish, why should they cherish other forms of creation?

So raising consciousness of God in creation happens only as we raise consciousness of God in ourselves. As this happens, we realise that to cherish God's creation is as basic to the Christian life as breathing.

Celtic Challenge

Illtyd (fifth century) left his soldier's career after he was converted and sought God alone. As he prayed a voice said, 'When you get up tomorrow go straight to the wooded valley to the west where you will find the place you are to make your home. This is God's will for you, for this place is convenient, fertile and suitable for human dwelling.' Illtyd arrived to find a valley watered by springs from which brooks flowed into the river.

The local ruler discovered while hunting that Illtyd had tamed a wild deer. He was so impressed by this sign of his spiritual presence that he granted him a wider area of land and asked him to develop a Christian community and school for all ages. Illtyd laid before Bishop Dubricius plans for a unique community of Christians that would combine prayer, leadership training and agricultural development. But the humans outgrew the farm space needed to provide for them and for the many visitors, so one day Illtyd asked a group to pray with him for the extension of the community's grounds.

They called the whole community to prayer and walked to the shore at low tide, when the sea used to withdraw a mile or two. Illtyd marked a line near the shore with his staff and in the name of God forbade the water to pass that mark again. The result was that they were able to cultivate much land reclaimed from the sea, which produced abundant crops.

Illtyd used to withdraw at regular intervals to a cave by the river Ewenny to seek God alone. He slept on a cold stone and lived on barley loaves and fish. Sometimes he made retreat at Llanhamlach, five kilometres to the east of Brecon, where the horse that brought his provisions was accompanied by a stag who inspired the horse to go at a gallop!

Illtyd was famed as a God-inspired steward of the earth.

He invented a much improved method of ploughing. 'Seed multiplied and toil met with abundant reward' says an ancient account.

Illtyd was a great teacher. His method was to combine spirit, mind and body in a harmony. He divided students into twenty-four groups, each responsible for one hour's worship and adoration, so that ceaseless praise would flow to God. The intellectual side involved instruction in the 'seven sciences', the best knowledge the times could offer. Physical well-being was fostered by clearing the land, digging and ploughing. Great future leaders such as Samson, Gildas, David and Paul Aurelian were trained there.

Hearing of a famine in what is now Brittany, Illtyd loaded a boat with much needed seed corn. It is said that, at the end of his life, he joined his former pupil Samson at the great Christian community at Dol. Here Samson carried on in the spirit of his teacher. They planted a big orchard of fruit trees, three miles long, reaching from Dol to Cai.

For our early Christians and churches, faith and prayer were connected with the earth. And churches are reconnecting today. The video *Transformations** includes the story of the town of Almolongua, Guatemala, which was gripped by acute poverty, violence, and witchcraft. Crop yields were low owing to arid land and poor working habits. Following the humbling and uniting of the town's church leaders, who called the people to concerted prayer, over 80 per cent became Christians. There was a social and agricultural transformation. They have planted more crops and improved the quality of the soil and the work. Now they yield large vegetables which are sold many miles away. Radishes harvest in 40 instead of 60 days, and there are

*Gateway Publications, PO Box 11905, London NW10 4ZQ

up to three harvests of some crops. The town has been nicknamed America's vegetable garden. US researchers came to learn the secret. Local Christians believe it is the wisdom God gave to them as they become intimate with him.

Do I have to choose between justice and holiness?

Question

I belong to an evangelical church, and work for an urban soul-project which reaches out to drug addicts and marginalised peoples. Some people in my church criticise me. They say we are wasting our time and should be telling these people to repent and accept Jesus. People in the project hate that approach. They say it turns them off and I should leave the church.

Why do some Christians make such a fuss about personal morality when people are rotting in the streets – surely those are the big issues? There's a clash between the holiness and the justice traditions. Which should I follow?

Response

King David loved God and wanted to be in right relationship with him. He also wanted right relations between people – which requires fair treatment. In the Bible the word 'righteousness' means both holiness and justice.

Celtic Challenge

Aidan encouraged his sponsor, King Oswald, to take practical action to care for the most needy. As far as we know, Oswald was the first English ruler to appoint a member of staff whose role was to care for the poor. It was the beginning of a social revolution. And we know that when that staff member informed Oswald, when he and his guests were enjoying an Easter Day banquet, that a crowd of hungry people were outside, Oswald ordered their own food to be taken to them, and also the silver dishes to be broken into pieces and distributed to the poor. Aidan was so moved that he raised the king's arm and prophesied that it would long be blessed. If Aidan was given money by rich people he would give it to the poor, or go to the slave market and buy a slave his freedom. He had the courage to challenge rich people who misused their wealth or power. Yet Aidan lived a ceaseless rhythm of prayer and meditation – he was a holy man. For Aidan, prayer, evangelism and justice all flowed from the heart of God.

Why don't some people get healed when they are prayed for?

Question

Why is it that some people are not healed when they are prayed for?

Response

There are combinations of reasons.

Jesus heals and calls us to heal the sick (Luke 9:1). Jesus also wants us to do this with discernment – sensing in what way he intends to manifest his healing grace in each situation. Jesus chose certain divine moments to identify a 'candidate' for healing and to heal in the right way at the right time. So maybe the healer is being insensitive.

God wants us to experience both suffering and healing. Paul says we are called to share in the suffering of creation (Romans 8: 22-23) and of the universal Body of Christ (1 Corinthians 12:24b-26). God has created a universe which is not individualistic. So, if we brainwashed individualistic westerners expect healing to be like a slot machine – the more prayer you put in the more healing you get out on demand for a particular person – we are falling into idols and illusions.

Our openness to God – light – love – trust – or our lack of it, can help or block the healing flow from our prayers for someone. Tension is a killer. A sick person needs to understand what is happening to their body and to their emotions – where the process has got to. Maybe we need to help them understand this process. Maybe the next step for the healing is acceptance.

So in CERTAIN cases lack of healing can be due to lack of faith. But never tell a person that is the cause – for that can condemn them to self-accusation that destroys.

My experience is that I am disappointed that X or Y is not healed and amazed that Z is healed after a healing ministry – God always seems to do something good. Our GP asked us to keep a record of answers to prayer from an intercession group that prayed for sick people who were not present. This record built our faith incredibly.

Celtic Challenge

Sometimes we can be too quick. Several healing stories of Celtic Christians record them praying for a dead or near dead person for several hours, combining this with artificial respiration, breathing on them etc.

Cuthbert, a promising young leader in a seventh-century faith community at Melrose was expected to die of plague along with many of his brothers. They held an all-night prayer vigil for his recovery. When he heard of this next morning he said, 'Then what am I lying here for? God will certainly have heard the prayers of so many good people.' He got up, and day by day his strength returned, but he had a limp for the rest of his life. His mentor and leader, Boisil, prophesied that Cuthbert would never again be struck by the same disease but that he himself would soon fatally succumb to it. So these two people, one healed and one not healed, spent the last week of Boisil's life learning together from John's Gospel. A good death can be a form of healing.

My boyfriend's not a Christian – should I marry him?

Question

I really love my boyfriend and I would like to get married but he says he doesn't see the point in getting married. He doesn't mind my being a Christian but he says he is not religious. He also says he doesn't want children.

Answer

The only direct advice I can find in the Bible is when the apostle Paul told Christian widows they were free to get married again but only to Christian men (1 Corinthians 7:39). Paul also advised Christians: 'Do not try to work together as equals with unbelievers, for it cannot be done' (2 Corinthians 6:14).

Try to get your head round your boyfriend's way of thinking. Why does he not want children? Is he afraid of responsibility? Or of bodily intimacy or of the processes of birth, growth and parenthood? Why not introduce him to Christian friends who have recently had a baby – acclimatise him to birth and nurture; let there be sharing and questions from the heart.

If he is frightened of self-sacrifice, what will happen to his relationship with you once you fail to satisfy some aspect of his life?

Try to communicate with him your love of Jesus. Forget religion – share deeply what your deepest loves are – yours and his.

In order for marriage to be a 'gift', each partner needs to be willing to let the other go. If either of you is possessive, marriage cannot work.

The key point about a relationship is an unconditional commitment to the other for better or worse. Is he willing to make that commitment to you? If so, can he see the value in making this public, so that no one else will try to usurp the relationship?

He may be right that an expensive wedding is unnecessary – but if he really loves you he will want to do what pleases you.

Celtic Challenge

Columba was a guest on Rathlin Island. The local ferryman came to see him. 'My wife finds me so ugly she will not lie with me and intends to leave me,' he confided. Columba met the wife and pleaded with her, but in vain. 'I'd rather be a nun than live with him,' she told him. Columba put forward a proposal: each of them should miss meals and pray alone about this matter for the rest of the day. They agreed. Columba himself prayed on through the night. Next day the wife met with Columba and her husband. 'I don't know what has happened to me,' she said, 'but the man I hated yesterday I love today. During the night my heart was changed from loathing to love.'

That story is about a husband, not a boyfriend, but does it give a clue as to how your boyfriend might be changed, too?

Why do Christians make sex the big issue?

Question

Older Christians make sex the big issue. Sometimes you'd think from the headlines that Christianity is about nothing else except the things they are against. Christians my age are more laid back. We love Jesus and want to accept anyone who's around. So what's the big deal?

Response

You are right, megaphone shouting is the worst possible context for exploring sensitive, personal matters such as sex. Many single people are lonely. We want friendship, trust, understanding, intimacy. We can't take being stereotyped and shouted at.

Question

Many young Christians think sex has been put into an antiquated 'Don't do this' framework of their parents' generation. Finding out for yourself, and doing what you feel, seems better. The film *Four Weddings and a Funeral* reflected a widespread belief that marriage is something wealthy hypocrites go through, whereas two people who commit to a relationship of trust do not need to enter into marriage. There's nothing in the Bible about not living together until you complete some legal formalities, is there? Where do Celtic Christians stand on this?

Celtic Challenge

Celtic-style Christians gently steer us out of the megaphone context into a 'desert' context. The 'desert' is a context where we can listen to one another, and trust and enjoy one another's company enough to want to listen and learn from one other. If we are still being aggressive or defensive in our attitudes we are not ready to explore this together.

However, the fact that this is a better context for exploring matters of sex does not mean that anything goes. A mentor or soul friend helps us to observe what happens after different kinds of experience.

In the Celtic Christian communities everyone was welcome as a friend, and accepted for who they were. People did not get their sense of identity from their sexuality, but from their being children of God and members of the human family.

Some people loved Christ so much that they chose to make a very personal sacrifice. Such people took either a vow of celibacy or a vow to have sex only within a life-long relationship of unconditional trust between a man and a woman who were open to the possibility of the gift of life.

Many young people, including Christians, say yes to sex because they are frightened to say no, rather than because they have a deep sense that this would be the fitting fulfilment of a relationship that has blossomed into unconditional commitment. Sex is only safe with a person who is able, within themselves, to say 'no.' The 'say no' movement among young Christians in the USA has now spread to other countries. Those who say 'no' pledge that they will remain virgins until they meet the person they feel called to love for the rest of their lives.

Why do Christians get screwed up about gays?

Question

Why do Christians get screwed up about gays?

Response

Christians who get screwed up about the gay debate usually have something to hide; it may be some part of their own sexual or power responses are not integrated with God. But lots of Christians who think same-sex acts are wrong are not screwed up.

God is like a mother hen who wants to gather all her chicks to her. We (and churches) should reflect this attitude. We gather, befriend, celebrate together with all God's children, whatever their size, colour and orientation. So a parent regards a child who falls in love with a profit-driven tycoon, and a child who falls in love with someone of the same gender, as still part of the family.

Morality is a good thing, but it is not the point. The point is to move with God and into God. The servant is kept in check by morals; the family member gets the key to the car.

The question now becomes, how do we relate to family members whom we believe are going wrong? Here is one example of a dialogue:

Two friends, one straight and the other gay, explored the subject of gay sex. The straight guy said 'I have tried to put myself in your shoes. If I was in your shoes, I honestly believe that I would explore more ways of experiencing intimacy and touch, but, to be crudely frank, I believe the penis is made for the vagina, not for the rectum, so I would refrain from using it in this way either as a heterosexual or a homosexual. I believe this for several reasons: the Bible, nature and the experience of those who do this. It is not the biological purpose of these organs to use them that way, so they violate nature. But also, as with heterosexual penetration, this creates a soul- as well as a body-bond. There is a tearing when it ends. Each tearing creates more fragmentation of the body-soul person. However, if you sincerely believe that the Holy Spirit wants you to do this, and if it makes you more whole, I would be open to think again. I do not stop being friends with you, if you can respect my convictions about this.'

Question

But being gay isn't just about having sex, is it?

Response

No. Some define gay as 'Good As You'. Gays have been made to have a low self-image and are making the point that they are not inferior. The Christian treats everyone as a person. A low self-image in anyone, hetero- or homosexual, can be healed. Others define gay as happy, exuberant, creative – hence gay celebrations. Christians should take time with one another to release the wellsprings of repressed creativity. Those whose energies are not channelled in having a family often make glorious contributions to human life. But releasing and celebrating creativity is best done together by people of all orientations.

Celtic Challenge

Celtic Christians believe that marriage, which is open to the possibility of a third life even when this is not possible in practice, reflects God's nature – Three-in-One Love. This is known as the Trinity. If the Trinity was just 'the Father' and 'Jesus' it would be an ingrown love. The third Person, the Spirit, pours out God's love into every person and place and makes it outgoing, unselfish and, above all, creation of new life. Sexual relations between two people of the same sex cannot reflect the nature of Divine Love in the same way. Two people of the same gender are not designed to bring a third person to birth nor to be complementary in the way that heterosexuals are. Celtic Christians believe God speaks through creation as well as through the Bible. Nature gives us common sense insights into what is healthy or otherwise. Take one example: the lining of the rectum is more fragile than the lining of the vagina. It ruptures and bleeds more easily; it is not designed for sexual intercourse.

This does not mean that two people of the same gender can't have a deep, committed relationship. Nor does it mean that anyone has to hide their orientation. None of us should ever stereotype another person. The most important thing is that each person seeks to honour God and the other person in their deepest relationships.

'Christians are idolaters' – how do we answer this charge?

Question

Some evangelical churches have a notice board which says, 'We worship Jesus as Lord . . .' A Muslim I work with says that is idolatry – there is only one God and all people should worship him alone, not a human being. What should I say to him?

Response

Those notice boards are an example of how some Protestants have taken Jesus out of the Trinity. Jesus warned people against worshipping him as a human being, and Christians believe that Jesus was fully a human being.

Christians also believe that Jesus was fully divine – but we have a responsibility to make clear that we worship only God, not a human being. That is why we should not cut Christ out of the Trinity as if he were on his own, apart from the Creator and the Spirit. I encourage these churches to replace those notice boards. Let them state 'We worship one God, revealed in Christ.'

Celtic Challenge

You O Father, with your only Son and the Holy
Spirit are God.
You are God, one and immortal;
God, incorruptible and unmoving;
God, invisible and faithful;
God, wonderful and worthy of praise;
God, strong and worthy of honour;
God, most high and magnificent;
God, living and true;
God, wise and powerful;
God, holy and splendid;
God, great and good;
God, awesome and peace-loving;
God, beautiful and righteous;
God, pure and kind;
God, blessed and just;
God, tender and holy.

You are God, not in the singularity of one
person, but in the trinity of one substance.

We believe in you;
we bless you;
we adore you;
and we praise your name for evermore.

From the Stowe Missal *– the service book used in the monastery of Tallaght, Ireland, in the eighth to ninth century.*

Are ikons idols or aids?

Question

The Bible says, 'You shall not worship or bow down to engraved images' (Exodus 20:4). Aren't Christians who use ikons, candles etc. doing exactly that?

Response

This issue was massively debated in the Christian Church in the eighth century.

Idols were banned in the Old Testament because people got their fix from them instead of from God. They lived their lives through these images of another being – so they were not free to be truly themselves.

In the fullness of time Christ was sent to be a physical ikon of the invisible God. Thus it became clear that God could use a material body to point to eternal reality and that God intended created things to be pointers to the invisible God (Romans 1:20).

Humans are made in the likeness of God and are therefore co-creators. Creative arts are part of the creation that God blesses.

Ikons point away from themselves to God. Idols draw us away from God to themselves.

> To the pure all things are pure.
>
> *Titus 1:15*

Celtic Challenge

Early Irish and English faith communities developed creative arts studios – scriptoria – where writing and painting sacred texts and images were absorbing acts of meditation, during which the scribe might glimpse the divine. They prayed with ikons.

> Our artist-scribe undertook his physically and intellectually demanding labours on behalf of all Creation as a hermit, the book becoming his 'desert', like Christ in the wilderness and Cuthbert on Inner Farne. Cassiodorus said that each word written was a wound on Satan's body. This was the spiritual front-line . . . Glimpsing their mysteriously lit pages or covers could change lives.
>
> Painted Labyrinth: The world of the Lindisfarne Gospels, *Prof. Michelle P. Brown (British Library, 2003)*

Symbols and all that – aren't they just froth?

Question

At my girlfriend's church, people make banners with symbols such as lions, white horses and rainbows. They wave these around. The pastor of my church says that sort of thing is dangerous and is all froth. How can I know the truth of this matter?

Response

In order to know whether this is dangerous and should be avoided, we need to know how God has designed human beings. We know from research that there are different personality types. Some people perceive life in pictures, others in ideas or words. We read about both types in the Bible.

John, who was exiled to Patmos Island because of his steadfast Christian faith, was caught up by the Holy Spirit in a vision while he was praying one Sunday. This vision, which now forms the Bible Book of Revelation, contains symbols that include horses, a lamb, sea and rainbows. Such symbols have always been used by Christians. The apostle Paul, on the other hand, uses words more than symbols, though he uses word pictures such as the human body.

> If you hear something, you forget it.
> If you see something, you remember it.
> If you do something, you understand it.
>
> *Principles of the Nuffield Organisation.*

Celtic Challenge

Is it all froth? It could be. The Celtic Challenge consists in taking the symbol that most speaks to your condition, and practising daily how to live out its meaning.

Take, for example, the cross. As a girl, Brigid of Ireland went to sleep with her arms stretched out in the shape of the cross because she wanted to keep praying while she slept!

Once she was with a pagan man who was dying. She longed to help him understand what it meant for God to send him a Saviour. So she picked rushes out of the floor mat and made them into a distinctive form of cross which helped her tell the dying man the story of Christ's death. He accepted Christ into his life before he died.

Brigid crosses became a byword. On the first day of the Celtic Spring (February 1) it has become a custom to make Brigid crosses and hang them in places which have become cobwebbed or prey to unsavoury influences during the untended dark winter months, as a way of welcoming the light and presence and victory of Christ into that place.

Do sermons have to put people off God?

Question

My new pastor preaches that Jesus is the only Saviour, and if you don't have him, you are damned. Now several church members have given up Christianity because of the way he puts over his views. Is there a better way?

Response

Orthodox Christianity believes in one God who is Creator, Saviour and Sustainer.

The heart of God, so to speak, is a communion of three Loves: one Love is always creating and sending; one Love is always pouring into human life to liberate it – and even once went to the extremity of Love and poured into a woman's womb in order to become one of us; the third Love is always connecting up the other Loves to every person, place and thing.

The second Love is saving us – each of us personally and the world as a whole – from the fragmentation and alienation that comes when our egos try to work against the divine flow of things.

This pattern is the way reality is, whatever one's culture or creed.

God the Saviour is carrying people to the Father whether they can yet put a name to him or not. The only 'winning' way to preach is with tears.

Celtic Challenge

Cuthbert's sermons moved people to open up their hearts to him. He often shed tears of compassion when preaching and when celebrating Holy Communion:

> He offered his prayer to the Lord not by raising his voice but by shedding tears which sprang from the depths of his heart . . .
>
> Great numbers came to him. They confessed their sins, confided in him their temptations, and laid open to him the common troubles of humanity they were labouring under . . . no one left unconsoled, no one had to leave carrying the burdens they came with. Spirits that were chilled with sadness he could warm back to hope again. Those beset with worry he brought back to thoughts of the joys of heaven . . .
>
> *From Bede's* Life of Cuthbert.

Why can't church leaders be 'of the people'?

Question

Why can't bishops and church leaders be 'one of us' like pop stars, footballers and Princess Diana – or Jesus for that matter?

Response

They can. When the church became a big, successful organisation, out-of-touch academics were too often appointed as church leaders through the old-boy network. But that is changing fast. It was not always like that, and it won't be like that in the future

Celtic Challenge

A senior officer in the Roman army named his son Martin, which means warrior, and determined to make him into a top soldier. While Martin was still a boy, they were sent from their home town in Hungary to do duty in Italy. One day Martin ran for shelter during a thunderstorm and found himself in a church service. He was captivated by a story of Jesus, and by the Christians' care of people with learning difficulties, and decided to become a Christian.

Before Martin had completed his instruction for baptism his father presented him to the Emperor, and the tall, strong young adult was sent to do military service in France. On his arrival at Amiens Martin, in uniform and on a horse, passed a beggar who was freezing in the cold. Moved with compassion, Martin took off his fine cloak, cut it in half, and gave one half to the beggar. That night he had a dream. Jesus stood by his bed and said: 'Martin, you have done a great act of love for me. I was cold and you gave me half your cloak.' Martin dressed, went to the nearest church, woke the priest, and asked to be baptised.

After twenty years serving in the army as a Christian, Martin went to the Emperor and, braving his anger, persuaded him to release him from the army so that he could serve God without any pay. He offered his help to Bishop Hilary of Poitiers, who ordained him a deacon, but Hilary was soon to be exiled by the Arian heretics who gained control of the church.

Martin walked many days to visit and win over his parents. His mother joyfully became a Christian, but his father, whose pride was hurt, turned him out. So Martin, who longed to seek God in solitude, set up a cell first in Milan, and then, accompanied by a friend, on the island of Gallineria. There they had little more than roots of various plants to live on. Once he almost died of poisoning, but was healed through his own prayer of faith.

In 361 Martin returned to Hilary, who had been reinstated, and Hilary encouraged him to set up a group of cells around some property he had at Ligugé. So began a unique experiment in community. A fellowship of prayer, evangelism and service to the poor grew up, founded on mutual trust and discipline. It was said to be the first monastic community in Europe.

Martin lived for God alone, but that meant living also for others. One day he tended a leper, another he prayed for hours over a man who had hanged himself, and whose life returned. A madman was cured. God's power was mightily at work in him.

Young Christians left their compromising urban churches and streamed to Martin, where they sought out marginalised country dwellers who knew nothing of Christianity. Martin's community taught them agricultural skills as well as the Bible. They loved the ordinary people and healed the sick. Admittedly Martin did sometimes physically destroy shrines of pagan idols (unlike Christian leaders in Britain) but often he would win the pagans round and they themselves would help him dismantle these.

It was not surprising that, when the neighbouring Bishop of Tours died in 372, all the people were determined to make Martin their next bishop. He agreed, on condition that he sat on a cow stool instead of a throne at his consecration, and that he could continue to live a simple life under vows at a quiet place a little apart from Tours. From there Martin made evangelistic visits to pagan villages. He used his privilege of being a guest at the Emperor's table to ask for the release, before he ate anything, of innocent prisoners in Tours. The Emperor deeply respected Martin's Christian example.

Can you give words of wisdom to a 'wet behind the ears' youth minister?

Question

Have you any advice for a young, still learning, still 'wet behind the ears' youth minister? I am a Baptist, still at university, and after reading a few books, I am very, very interested in Celtic Christianity, and have started calling myself a Celtic Christian. God has put a love in my heart for teenagers that I cannot put into words. I would dearly appreciate any words of wisdom you could give me.

Response

Daily meditate on a Scripture passage and a writing about one of the Celtic 'cloud of witnesses'. Learn to go 'into the desert' (i.e. to be still and alone, and also to learn about the desert fathers and mothers). Learn to weave together the strands of Christianity that have become separated.

Work out a rhythm of prayer, work and recreation for each day and week. Become transparent with a soul friend about everything – e.g. feelings, hopes, frustrations, money, sex, power, what to learn.

This love for teenagers that God has given you is very precious. One thing could destroy this ministry – letting it take you over. That is why you need the boundaries and disciplines of the desert. Also a vision and ethos for the emerging church that will provide lasting foundations for the future of the teenagers you minister to.

Celtic Challenge

Be helpful when you are at the bottom of the ladder and be the lowest when you are in authority. Be simple in faith but well trained in manners; demanding in your own affairs but unconcerned in those of others. Be guileless in friendship, astute in the face of deceit, tough in time of ease, tender in hard times. Keep your options open when there's no problem, but dig in when you must choose. Be pleasant when things are unpleasant, and sorrowful when they are pleasant. Disagree where necessary, but be in agreement about the truth. Be serious in pleasures but kindly when things are bitter. Be strong in trials, weak in dissensions . . .

Be friendly with people of honour, stiff with rascals, gentle to the weak, firm to the stubborn, steadfast to the proud, humble to the lowly. Always be sober, chaste, modest. Be discreet in duty, persistent in study, unshaken in turmoil, valiant in the cause of truth, cautious in time of strife. Be submissive to good, unbending to evil, gentle in curiosity, untiring in love, just in all things. Be respectful to the worthy, merciful to the poor. Be mindful of favours, unmindful of wrongs. Love ordinary people, and don't crave for riches, but cool down excitement and speak your mind.

Obey your seniors, keep up with your juniors, equal your equals, emulate the perfect. Don't envy your betters, or grieve at those who surpass you, or censure those who fall behind, but agree with those who urge you on. Though weary, don't give up. Weep and rejoice at the same time out of zeal and hope. Advance with determination, but always fear for the end.

Columbanus – a letter to a young disciple.

Other Books by Ray Simpson

The Celtic Prayer Book in four volumes (Kevin Mayhew Ltd):
Vol 1: Prayer Rhythms: Fourfold Patterns for Each Day
Vol 2: Saints of the Isles: A Year of Feasts
Vol 3: Healing the Land: Natural Seasons, Sacraments and Special Services
Vol 4: Great Celtic Christians: Alternative Worship
Church of the Isles: A Prophetic Strategy for Renewal (with group study guide) (Kevin Mayhew Ltd)
Celtic Daily Light (new edition) (Kevin Mayhew Ltd)
Exploring Celtic Spirituality New Study Guide edition (Kevin Mayhew Ltd)
CD – Celtic Journey with Ray Simpson (Kevin Mayhew Ltd)
The Joy of Spiritual Fitness (Zondervan UK)
Before We Say Goodbye: Preparing a Good Death (HarperCollins)
A Holy Island Prayer Book (Canterbury Press/Morehouse)
Celtic Blessings (Loyola Press, USA)
Soulfriendship: Celtic Insights Into Spiritual Mentoring (from St Aidan Press)
Give Yourself a Holy Island Retreat (St Aidan Press)
Celtic Spirituality: Rhythm, Relationships and Roots (Grove Books)

The Community of Aidan and Hilda
Registered Charity 1055306
The Open Gate, Holy Island, Berwick-upon-Tweed,
TD15 2SD
Tel + 01289 389222
theopengate@theopengate.ndo.uk
www.aidan.org.uk

Books distributed by St Aidan Press are available from the above address.

FURTHER READING

Meeting Emma: A Story of Spiritual Discovery by Michael Spyker (Open Book Publishers, Halifax Street, Adelaide, South Australia, 5000)

A young spiritual seeker named Emma chances to meet Joe, a middle-aged evangelical college lecturer who is willing to accompany Emma on her search with an open mind. They explore things like contemplative prayer, sacred space, creative art, symbols, holy leisure, thin places, soul friends and values. An appendix provides spiritual exercises that enable the reader to engage with these realities for themselves.

Atonement for a Sinless Society by Steve Chalke (Paternoster Press)

Exploring Celtic Spirituality: Historic Roots for Our Future study guide edition by Ray Simpson (Kevin Mayhew Ltd)